IT HAPPENS
WITH GURKHAS

IT HAPPENS WITH GURKHAS

TALES FROM AN ENGLISH NEPALI, 1944–2015

J.P. CROSS

The History Press

I dedicate this book to my Gurkha comrades in arms in war and near war, near peace and in peace, for more than seventy years. Thank you for your comradeship, steadfastness and life-saving devotion to duty, all of which I have tried to reciprocate. You have made my life fuller and more purposeful than has been the lot of many, many others and of this I am humbly and proudly aware. Thank you.

Cover illustrations: Front: A group of Gurkha trainees; Rear: A parliamentary delegation visits the Jungle Warfare School in 1969.

First published 2016

The History Press
The Mill, Brimscombe Port
Stroud, Gloucestershire, GL5 2QG
www.thehistorypress.co.uk

British Library Cataloguing in Publication Data.
A catalogue record for this book is available from the British Library.

ISBN 978 0 7509 6636 8

Typesetting and origination by The History Press
Printed and bound in Great Britain by TJ International

Contents

Foreword

The Gurkhas are different from other regiments because their interests and backgrounds are so diverse. They must acquire fluency in another language; they need to engage with and understand other religious faiths; and they have to embrace and admire a different culture. No British Gurkha officer has immersed himself more deeply in these opportunities than John Cross.

Nepal requires British soldiers who serve in the Gurkhas and wish to become Nepali citizens to renounce their British citizenship. John Cross is only the second to have completed the course, and the first man and first former British officer to have done so. Today he lives in Pokhara, in western Nepal, adjacent to the British Gurkhas' selection centre, where newly commissioned British Gurkha officers come to learn the language and culture of the soldiers they will command. John Cross lectures to them every year. He inspires them with the love of Nepali culture that has shaped his life, while not losing sight of their roles as soldiers.

The stories in this book reveal a love of language and a sense of humour which pricks pomposity: Gurkhas are good at that. For them, and for those who know and love Nepal, John Cross is a legend in his own lifetime.

Sir Hew Strachan
Professor of International Relations
University of St Andrews

Introduction

In the introduction to my first book of articles, *Gurkha Tales*, I wrote that Gurkhas, certainly the older men and especially former soldiers, love telling stories. The habit of 'capping' stories is not confined to gnarled fingers grasping pint pots of ale in English pubs: one-time Gurkha warriors also manage to cap them just as well, if not better. As my father told me, 'Most stories have a cocked hat and a sword.'

In this second book of articles, reminiscences, essays – call them what you will – I have repeated the mixture as before, my limit being the amount of words allowed by the publishers. One aspect that troubles me is that many of the stories, far too many some will deem, contain 'me' more than any modest person should allow. However, my only excuse, were one needed, is that without me those stories would not have happened at all. So, warts and all, here they are.

The one major difference in Nepal between the time frame in which I produced *Gurkha Tales* and this book is that many villages that were thriving communities have had major population reductions. The twelve-year-long insurgency problem that drove many people from their traditional village habitats, the move to the towns for better education for children and permission for Gurkha ex-servicemen to live on a permanent basis in Britain are the three main reasons. I have kept the stories in this book from touching on any of these three points; likewise the massive earthquakes that took place in 2015 play no part.

One personal change to me has been the granting of Nepalese citizenship, a process that took thirty-two years, six months and two days. Rudyard Kipling's words about not trying to hurry the East stood me in good stead and patience was rewarded. The story of becoming only the second English Nepali is in the book: the first Briton, some fifty years ago, was an English lady, Ms Eileen Lodge, who founded the leprosarium, Green Pastures, not far from my house. Since then the granting of citizenship for some types of Nepalis as well as for foreigners has become exquisitely harder. Since becoming a Nepali, however, in spite of the staggering amount of joy and happiness shown even by those with whom I had never previously spoken, no more stories have eventuated.

The year 2015 was the 200th year of British–Gurkha military 'together-ness', as soldiers of the Honorable East India Company from 1815, then, from 1858 until 1947, the (pre-partition) Indian Army – there was never any military formation named the 'British–Indian Army' – and, since 1948, the British Army. In April I was the only pre-partition ex-member at the 200th anniversary of one of the three original regiments of 1815, the 1st Battalion of the 1st Gorkha Rifles. A description also appears in this book.

I shall be 91 when this book is published. 'Birthdays' are not traditionally observed by hill folk – most not knowing when the appointed day falls – and I have told my surrogate family not to bother about any of mine till I am 100! Even at 90 I have had to wear tunnel vision spectacles for more than one-third of my life; I have also lived with civilian Nepalis and military Gurkhas for more than seventy years, slightly more than one-third of our combined military life. Had either been prophesied when I was a youngster I would probably have thought such a prophecy madness as well as thoroughly frightening. As Camus put in *The Plague*, 'one grows out of pity when it's useless' and self-pity was never on my menu. I spoke to ex-king Gyanendra in 2013 and told him how sorry I still was that I could not personally thank his late elder brother how much I appreciated his gift of permanent residential status and being an authorised land and house owner (the only foreigner in Nepalese history so honoured) which had made the late autumn of my life so happy. 'Sarkar,' I said, using the correct protocol word had he still been king, 'I have a request. When you get back home, please go to your family shrine and personally thank your late elder brother for his kindness to me.'

A lovely smile spread over the ex-king's face. 'Of course I will,' he said.

I know that without the late king's benevolence and without either of those two mathematical unthinkables many of the stories in these pages would never have come to be written.

I hope you enjoy reading this book as much as I enjoyed writing the composite pieces.

J.P. Cross
Pokhara
June 2016

In the Beginning

'Thirteen, unlucky for some!' is a cry tombola fans know well. I do not count fear of the number thirteen, 'triskaidekaphobia' to the buffs, as one of my many weaknesses but recently it did just cross my mind to take note of it. You may wonder why.

Well, apart from being reported dead three times in three months during my nearly thirty-eight years of military service in Asia, I have been shot at from 4 yards in front and less than that behind, nearly had my head cut off twice – once by an angry Iban armed with a Japanese sword and once by an even angrier Gurkha armed with a kukri – as well as been threatened from 3ft away by a mad Gurkha who had a loaded and cocked rifle with the safety catch off, inches from my navel. I have had a price put on my head twice and received two death threats, one by post and the other by word of mouth – all in so-called peacetime. Any self-respecting cat might well be jealous at my score of twelve.

In my middle years of soldiering I found I was 'ploughing a lonely furrow, often against the grain' by qualities that fitted me for an arduous and unconventional type of life, often with strange people whose upsurge of confidences and friendliness were reward in themselves, and often away from the crowd – a life remote and austere but one that I found infinitely more satisfying than the shallower, more conventional, surface-skating rat race that so many of my more successful peers preferred. Comfort, a large salary or even promotion in themselves had no particular attraction.

But not only that: the towering vantage points of hindsight and passing time have let me see many aspects of my unusual life in Asia in a different, possibly controversial, light and I don't want to waste the time spent away from the land of my birth in letting it all sink without trace.

Before the next, and possibly final, report of my death – after all, how long can one person's luck last? – it struck me that now was a good time to put on record my peculiar findings as well as some of the strange and unreasonable happenings that came my way during those years.

My stamping grounds went from the North-West Frontier of India, later to become Pakistan, over to Hong Kong and zigzagged south, through Indo-China and Burma, down into Malaya and across to the Borneo Territories – 'south-east Asian rain forest terrain' – with ten of the first thirty years spent under the jungle canopy when all the months, weeks and days are added together. Since 1976 I have lived in Nepal. Even though I still fail to understand much of Asian life, I have come to accept it. What in Europe is seen as Sod's Law is seen in Asia as God's Law, leaving plenty of banana skins for the unwary, the ignorant or the plain bloody-minded to slip on. After all, 'Asia' is a four-letter word.

The first thirty-eight years were in the army with Gurkhas – with nary a home posting, surely a British Army record? – in countries with a Muslim king, a Buddhist king, a Hindu king, an atheist communist prince and, in my earliest days overseas, the Christian and (very) British king emperor in India – or at least his representative the viceroy. I even had a letter of introduction to Lord Wavell, 'Give this to Archie,' murmured my great uncle Stephen Phillimore, his classmate, when I went to say goodbye to him on my pre-embarkation leave. Years later I threw it away unopened.

I was neither old enough to vote nor to marry when, as a lance corporal, I was detailed to go to India for officer training in mid 1944, a great help to my New Year's resolution of saving £1 from my pay each month. Troops, garnered from many countries and geared for most conditions, had started their invasion over the English Channel the day before my group of potential officers embarked on our month's voyage away from the cold-climate European theatre of war into a much, much hotter Asian theatre with Burma soon to be centre stage.

Despite lectures on what we might expect to find in India and lessons in elementary Urdu, the Indian Army's all-embracing 'Esperanto', when we arrived in Bombay after a month on board an overcrowded troopship, our initial reaction was one of disbelief at the diversity of it all, the cultural shock of the unknown and the incongruous. Could we get used to it? We wanted to and, eventually, did.

Our officer training took place in the Indian Military Academy (IMA), in Dehradun. The camp was superb, set in spacious grounds made wonderfully green by the monsoon rain. After the cramped conditions at sea, our quarters seemed palatial and being looked after by a bearer was a welcome sign of elevation from being 'one of the rank and file'.

During our training we found what the old lags had said was true, 'The scene changes, but the music never.' For elementary subjects we were taken in hand by gnarled British warrant officers and sergeants who told us that, 'When in Rome you do as India does. Get it?' And get it we did. Officers taught us tactics and jungle warfare. Only as training progressed did earlier lectures on the Indian Army penetrate my insular mind and begin to make sense as different peoples were produced in the flesh and I began to be able to tell one type of person from another by sight. It had never occurred to me that the majority of India's millions did not speak Urdu as their first language and, initially, I found that very hard going.

I first met Gurkhas as 'exercise enemy' when we went out for field and jungle training. They immediately attracted my attention as superb people but I feared a language barrier and an inadequacy of personal performance to match theirs. Six weeks or so from the end of our course we were asked which army, British or Indian, we wished to be commissioned in and to give three regiments we would like to join. I really had no idea, so I sought advice from the company second-in-command, a man called Griffiths. Although I might be one of those about whom it could be said that his men would follow him if only out of curiosity, he told me to try not to go to a British unit as any experience in the Indian Army would stand me in good stead. However, I was advised not to go into the Gurkhas as linguistically I was not even up to speaking Urdu let alone having to learn a second language, Nepali. So I put my name down to join an Urdu-speaking Indian regiment, dismissing the idea of Gurkhas entirely. In the event I was commissioned into the British Army but seconded to the 1st Gurkha Rifles (1 GR).

Having left England on 8 July 1944, I thought one day I'd have a return ticket. Now, in my 92nd year, I find I don't need one as I am still with Gurkhas and am now a nonagenarian citizen.

Sunday

Kathmandu, End of Monsoon 1984

Sunday, the first working day of the Nepalese week, starts this cloud-laden monsoon morning as on any other – cocks crowing, from 4 a.m., dogs barking and, in the zoo, the tigers roaring their sad threnody of caged despair. By 5 a.m. it is fully light and the valley wakes up.

The valley is ringed by hills that stand some 3,000ft higher, at around the 7,500ft mark. Nestling in their lee are villages peopled by Tamangs, Magars and some Gurungs, all of whom have long since forgotten their tribal languages. They live as elsewhere in Nepal, houses separate from one another and surrounded by patches of cultivation – chiefly, at this time of year, maize. Below them, on the valley floor, the villages, peopled by Newars, Chhetris and Bahuns, are of a completely different character. They are heavily concentrated, with narrow, angled streets, and houses of three storeys, all joined together. Idols and shrines are fitted into odd corners, daubed and dabbed saffron and red, and are also imprinted on some of the paving stones with which the streets are built. There will be a main temple in a small *durbar* square and a tank made of slabbed stone, full of filthy water. Standpipes are now a feature

15

of these villages and, at the end of the monsoon, there is no shortage of water like there was for the period leading up to the arrival of the rains. At these standpipes the village maidens bring their copper vessels and queue for their turn to fill them for the meal that has to be cooked so that the man of the house can go to work, and the children to school, having fed. Later on in the day, if the sun comes out, the dry-dugged gammers will wash as there was too much of a scrimmage on the previous day, the Saturday, when the men who go to work during the week had time off for their ablutions.

These villages are mute witness to the violent history of the valley; compact and secure, housing more than 1,000 able-bodied men, they are built on ground overlooking the fields, forts against enemies fighting dynastic wars or just looking for plunder. Their angled streets would prevent an easy rush through and would be useful for blocking purposes or mounting counter-attacks. They also have the great advantage of leaving maximum space for cultivation. Now the scene is one of a large green sea of growing paddy with villages on the higher ground standing sentinel. However, as land prices soar beyond belief, plots near feeder and main roads are being sold for building, thus starting an erosion of the old pattern.

Beyond these villages is the Ring Road, built a decade or so ago by the Chinese. This neatly encircles the two towns of Kathmandu and Patan, divided by that very holy river, the Bagmati. Two generations ago the townsfolk would drink the river water but nowadays this is impossible, such is the pollution.

The low cloud, with its patches of drizzle, has lifted slightly by 6 a.m. On the side roads and in the gulleys, it is muddy. Small children and dogs start on their daily routine of recycling nature. On the Ring Road a few early morning travellers, dressed in some sort of raincoat or merely with the almost universal umbrella, go about their business: a relief for an overnight watchman; votive offerings of flowers being taken to a shrine; a couple of grave-faced, shaven-pated monks, robed in maroon and amber; two spindly-legged, *dhoti*-clad Indian plainsmen, pushing a flat-topped cart of fruit to their chosen selling place; some people waiting for the delivery of milk; and the occasional taxi. Some soldiers, mostly recruits, from the nearby barracks, double along under command of an NCO. When it is dry the squad will form up by the side of the road and then lie down to do various exercises, but today, in the all-pervading dampness, running is enough for them. Other soldiers, in a large lorry and a small Jeep-like vehicle, are also out practising driving. Some stalwarts are out jogging, a few of them from the Tibetan refugee camp, and the occasional older man, probably a retired army officer, takes his morning constitutional. Near the perennial springs, the large daily wash – hotels' linen in the main – starts. It may even dry.

By 7 a.m. the first news broadcast of the day can be heard. The flat-toned, monotonous voice of the reader blurts out from many of the houses, following a passer-by so closely he can hear its bulletin as he goes on his way. Apart from that, it is generally quiet.

There is a wide swathe of grass on both sides of the Ring Road, with warning notices proclaiming to the general public that no building is permitted within a specified distance, a copy of one of the last laws the British passed in India before independence. Cattle, untethered and untended, can be found on it any day. They graze happily, now that the days of parched fodder, or no fodder at all, are at an end. Some have a heavy piece of wood hanging from their neck to impede movement, a type of hobbling device. A few are disconsolately lonely and it could be those that have been let loose as a propitiation when a Brahmin dies. All look much sleeker than before. Little knots of goats and sheep are also to be found. With very few leeches to pester them or their herdsmen, life in the valley has some advantages over other places in the rest of the country at this time of year.

Sun peeps through the dispersing mist, revealing the lush green of growing paddy. The colour varies from a golden green, to a rich velvet green and then to a darker moss green. In places the smoothness is broken by clumps of 8ft-tall maize, the long leaves now becoming sere with the pods ripening. The old shrine of Swayambhunath, perched on top of its own sanctuary-like hill, glints. Whoever decided to build it where it is was a genius, so well and ethereally does it fit into the landscape. It, to the south of the valley, and Bodhnath, to the north, both command a good view of the fields; it is said that no animal may plough within sight of these two shrines. True or false, ploughing is seldom done by animals in the valley; heavy-handled mattocks, bent backs and strong arms are still the order of the day.

In the town the day seems to start later than in the villages. Shops are open until late at night and many do not open again till 10 a.m., which invites a later start. Street sweepers do what they can against the mud and filth, mendicants beg for food at house doors, stray dogs scavenge and children start to play in the streets. Nowadays, with the spread of transistor radios, videos, television and of education, there are different ways of passing an evening than in previous years. On the whole, Kathmandu dwellers seem to go to bed later than their village counterparts. However, the children have as unfettered a time as ever. They are never left on their own away from their immediate dwelling and an elder sister or a mother is not far away. In Nepal it is good to have a daughter before a son so that there is someone to look after a second child. On this morning one toddler escapes detection and comes out of a house to paddle in some of the puddles formed by the overnight rain. He sees a small and innocuous dog nearby and the inborn desire to chastise it is so strong that he looks for a weapon. He finds a tiny piece of gravel and, hardly able to walk straight so young is he, makes his way up to the dog and hurls the minute handful at it. So puny is the effort that, even had contact been made, it would have been unnoticed. But that youngster will be a chastiser of dogs all his days!

Apart from the Nepalese townsfolk, there is a goodly sprinkling of Indian merchants. One such comes out of his house, dressed in white *dhoti* and Gandhi hat. He looks neither to left nor right and, lifting his *dhoti* free from the wet ground, makes his way to a temple for his morning devotions. He returns a short while later, high stepping, tika-daubed and disdainful in his purified and virtuous isolation. Not far away, another Indian, of more humble origin, carries a flat tray of mangoes on his head as he goes to his pitch past a temple, the very temporal home for some not very spiritual monkeys. One realises that mangoes are being carried and it only needs a jump and a snatch for a juicy meal. It sidles up, warily eyeing both vendor and fruit, its intentions obvious. The vendor fears an attack and tries to get out of range quickly, but his load is such that haste is imprudent. The monkey paces him, tensing its muscles until, in desperation, the Indian puts his free hand up over the rim of the tray and picks out the first mango that comes to his fingers. The monkey continues to eye him – has this all happened before? – and as the vendor throws it away over the animal's head, it lollops off after it, with the Indian hurriedly moving off in the other direction, glad that his one-mango offering can be counted as a holy gesture rather than an act of self-protection. This little pantomime attracts no attention from the passers-by.

By 9 a.m., from the surrounding villages, a stream of workers and school children make their way in to either Patan or Kathmandu, picking their way around the dirtier patches on the narrow paths. By now the clouds have dispersed and a hot sun is blazing down. The men who are going in to work as peons in a bank, functionaries in a government office or even the local telephone exchange are overdressed in a coat over their traditional wrap-over tunic, the *daura*, and jodhpur-like trousers, the *saruwal*. All wear the ubiquitous Nepali hat and, despite it being a tidy rig, it is unrealistically hot. To compensate for the heat from their coats and clothes designed to keep out the cold, they carry umbrellas, unfurled whatever the weather. Some will be dressed in white, mourning for a year the death of a close relative. Those whose work lies in humbler trades, such as carpentry or metalworking, wear sloppier, cooler clothes and go bareheaded. Many may still have a petal or two on their heads, showing that they have paid their religious respects for the day. Some of these people will have walked for two hours by the time they reach work: two hours there and two hours back – all for about £15 to £20 a month.

The schoolgirls are dressed tidily, in yellow, red, blue or white depending on which school they go to, all with well-oiled and beautifully combed hair. They walk demurely along, occasionally a ripple of laughter escaping their lips, all looking angelic, as though ghee would not dissolve on their tongues. Nothing but the Newari language is heard as these people move into town. The boys, also, for the most part, are in uniform, carrying their midday snack in a tiffin carrier, books in a satchel on their backs. Bolder than the girls, they take longer to get to school as they find a particularly muddy piece of ground to play in or another like-minded lad to play *khopi* with. This is a game throwing coins at one already on the ground, with the one that lands the nearest to it winning, as in bowls.

By 10 a.m. the main roads of the town are blocked with traffic. The police on point duty cope valiantly with the onslaught: waving arms and blowing whistles, as those better endowed than the villagers go to work. The amount of diesel fumes the policemen inhale in one day must be more than is good for them in one month, so dirty are most vehicles. Motorcyclists weave their way in and around the vehicles, as do many pushbikes, defying death, or courting it, reminiscent of the Japanese suicide pilots in the Second World War. And yet few stiffs or even hobblers are encountered! By 10.30 a.m. most of the staff have joined up with their desks and maybe even the man with the keys has come so that anything locked up overnight can be got out. Little groups of men form and disperse, only to reform, gossiping to their hearts' content, for isn't important work only done between 12 and 2?

In the streets, calm and bustle intermingle: a horoscope reader; a seller of trinkets, of farinaceous food-stuffs, of *biri* and betel; a few beggars and other paupers, pitifully distorted by unchecked disease, all squat with undignified resignation by the road; and, of course, the crowd, kaleidoscopically changing, always the same, as in any town anywhere.

Meanwhile, out in the fields the women start another phase of the day, now that breadwinner and children have left the house. For the most part this is weeding the rice crop, a woman's job; whatever else the menfolk do, it is not this. Valley folk are thin-legged men compared with the hill men; there are no hills to climb up and down, no heavy loads to be toted from afar. Not that life is easy, but it could be harder. Only the hewers and carriers of ever-precious firewood, brought from the valley rim, have legs fully muscled.

Near the weeding women flocks of egrets poke about for insects. How do they manage in the dry weather, when only one or two are ever seen? Now they are in their flocks of thirty and, at times, even of up to fifty. The expert will say that the only place in Europe that the egret can be found is in the Pripet marshes of south-east Poland. Here they are commonplace and of two main kinds – one almost white all over and one, less common, with more brown on head and neck. There is a saying among the Nepali elite, about anyone who is obviously better qualified than his peers, that he is an 'egret among the ducks'. But now both egret and duck are happy as they splash around for their more plentiful diet. In the River Bagmati, still greatly swollen by the rains, birds of prey gather around the corpse of some animal swept down in the spate and stuck on a sandbank.

In Kathmandu, past the international telephone exchange, the road falls away towards the stadium, where, later on in the day, devotees of soccer will be able to watch the final of the women's football competition, Pokhara versus Dharan. Taking a load of parsnips down this road in a rickshaw, the rider, a mere youth, does not see that his cargo is starting to fall out. One does fall and a woman, walking in the same direction, picks it up, gleeful in possessing something for nothing. A cyclist following the rickshaw shouts out that his load is falling and the driver tries to turn round and see, but his view is blocked by the width of the rickshaw and the canopy. As he tries to look from a wider angle, the rickshaw starts to swerve from side to side to such an extent that the rider can no longer control it. It overturns, narrowly being missed by a taxi, and the driver sprawls on the ground surrounded by parsnips. He picks himself up, shaken though unhurt, and starts to gather up his load. He then turns his attention to the rickshaw and finds it too heavy to right. The inevitable crowd has gathered and willing hands help him to right it. By the time the woman has reached the rickshaw, unnoticed by the youth who is still a bit dazed, one of the onlookers says, 'There she goes, taking the one that fell off farther up the road!' The youth looks up, sees her and makes a lunge at the parsnip that she is holding behind a package. She senses his coming, flinches and snarls at him, claiming the vegetable as her own. He snatches at it and regains it, triumphantly. Inconsistently – in that she is wearing red – he hisses at her, 'You green-clad widow!' and returns to his uncompleted task of repacking his load. She, for her part, angrily and proudly continues on her way, staring resolutely to her front.

Inside the bank where the foreigners have to go for their money, a gaggle of new-world, low-budget travellers turn the pages of the book in which the arrival of demanded money is written. None understand the inevitable two-week time lag between date expected and date announced. They are a motley crowd, unused to the heat and the dampness of monsoon conditions. They give off an aura of unwashed sadness that may belie some of them. The bank staff regard them with a tolerance born of familiarity. Some of them are very shabbily dressed, draggle-bearded and unkempt; they are a permanent target for small boys who now call all of European stock 'American', regardless of snubs, snarls or smiles they may get in return. Where these foreigners go on leaving the bank is a mystery – like flies in winter.

By noon, all the very important people are busy, ensconced in lordly isolation in upstairs offices, all aware of the responsibilities with which they are entrusted and all keeping a fine balance between prospect, probity and policy. In outer offices deferential subordinates diligently apply themselves, ready in an instant to answer the desk bell that rings when higher authority demands their presence. This tempo is kept up till 2 p.m., when the important go to meetings with other important ones and the lesser minions revitalise their severely depleted vitality with glasses of over-sweet and lukewarm tea.

Life unwinds gradually until around 5 p.m., when the morning rush begins in the other direction. The sun has gone in, the clouds hang low and menacing, and it starts to drizzle. The crowd converging on the stadium to see the women's football final brings near-pandemonium in the vicinity, but slowly conditions return to what goes for normal and, by 6.30, the roads are as empty as they were before the homeward rush started – with the Pokhara Ladies justly proud of their muddy victory over their rivals from Dharan.

The women toilers have returned from the fields, tired and wet, to prepare the evening meal for the ever-hungry throng. The breadwinner gets home and relaxes. After being fed, the children huddle up to a lamp and do their homework, men gather out of the rain in twos and threes and gossip, and the women are just thankful that yet another day, when so much has to be packed in to keep the minimum momentum needed to sustain life, is nearing its end.

Then it is bed time and, for those who live near the zoo, the roar of the tigers – driven to distraction in their small cages by a day-long inquisitive, teasing crowd of onlookers – joins the shrill and never-ending barking of the dogs, so, however tired people may be, they are forcibly reminded that, though another day is over, the night is still young.

Morning Walks

'Grandfather, take out one of your eyes.' The command was imperious and insistent; its deliverer was a tousle-haired 9-year-old Nepali boy, with authority well beyond his years, clearly leader of the cluster of kids with him. Surrender or walk on regardless? I was two hours from home and not quite halfway round one of the circuits of my morning walks. I looked at them, all with eyes button-bright and overflowing enthusiasm: how many other mid octogenarians would be similarly challenged?

I suppose the morning walk habit started when I was in Laos, living alone. On high days and holidays I would take my dog, Singha, my pedometer showing me that I walked between 21 and 28 miles. In my early days I would take language cards and I would ask people I met a question from the top word in the pile. They would be surprised to be asked if they caught crabs in the swamp or what noise their buffalo made when scratched. I was only accepted without hostility or suspicion when people learnt I was neither French nor American but a *khon Añgit*, an Englishman.

I met Pathet Lao patrols as I ranged far and wide. After the communists had taken over, every morning, everywhere, the ritual of political indoctrination would take place. One Saturday morning, early, miles out in the sticks and still a bit chilly, I saw an armed group of young Pathet Lao soldiers – looking for all the world like our Gurkhas – sitting cross-legged in a circle in a harvested rice field on the outskirts of the village they were garrisoning, being lectured by a hard-faced 'cadre'. They were directly in the line I was taking. I did not deviate but kept on towards them. I talked to Singha, in Nepali, telling him not to chase the goats or the pigs. The soldiers saw me coming, then heard a strange language. The cadre stopped talking, turned and stared at me, as did the soldiers, scowling severely. I sensed tension in the air but, having committed myself, chose to ignore it.

I walked into the centre of the group and told the dog to sit, give me one paw and then the other. He obliged me. In Lao I said to the group, 'That's discipline. That's how you won the war. Without it that's how you'll lose the peace.' I pointed to Singha. 'You can call him the "little soldier" but don't call me the "big dog".'

Blank amazement greeted this utterly unexpected stricture. Nothing existed in the book of rules for such behaviour that was neither hostile nor rude, merely eccentric. I wobbled my hands and knees, then my eyebrows and ears, asking the soldiers if they could. They burst out laughing, all semblance of severity gone. I put my arm round the shoulders of the cadre, a Vietnamese, my hand on his head and made a squeaking noise with my mouth. He gave a start but stayed silent. Such an occurrence was evidently not yet a common experience.

'You've got a mouse in your head,' I said sympathetically and inanely. 'I hope it doesn't hurt. And you teach politics?' By then I had gone as far as I dared so, telling the dog to follow me, turned and left without looking behind. For a brief moment I felt mighty cold on the back of my neck. I never heard anything about that trivial, unnecessary and entirely unrehearsed incident.

Once I had started living in Pokhara, in 1986, I only started walking after we began to keep dogs. With dogs, the morning walk habit set in properly. The dogs loved it: we had two. Three neighbours' dogs joined us to make five and the most I ever had trailing behind me was seven.

'Morning walk', along with 'half brain' and 'love marriage' are Nepali neologisms – 'paper wedding', to aid foreigners' citizenship process, is another fairly new one. No, I will not put words into your mouth by conflating the first two.

By now I have, on a conservative estimation, walked more than 100,000km, more than three times round the world at the equator. It was on one of our earlier walks when Buddhiman (my surrogate son) and I were wondering how much or how little the countryside had changed in the past 500 years when the idea of historical novel writing occurred to me.

When I was struggling with any passage in the book I was writing – for instance when I had nearly had the hero killed halfway through and felt I had to have him rescued, even though the scene I had set did not allow it – 'Winking little thoughts into my tiddlecup', unquote *Lolita*, I would drift for two or three hours mulling over a number of possible scenarios. Then suddenly, bingo, an answer would come.

On one walk in an unusual place in my early days I was heckled, rather rudely, by some schoolboys. I was, as normal, wearing shorts and traditional Nepali headgear. I did not answer them. I was chi-iked again and did not answer. I then heard an interesting comment from one of the boys: 'I thought he was a foreigner but he must be a Nepali because he refuses to talk to us.'

Twice I have limped back to the house bitten and bleeding, once when attacked, from either side, by two dogs and once when I found myself in the middle of our dog and a neighbour's fighting: anti-rabies jabs both times.

Buddhiman and I have seen pine martens, ferret badgers, mongooses and, once, a badger. Twice we have seen either a leopard or a tiger in the flesh and, separately, their droppings. Then the dogs seemed almost to walk on tiptoe, directly behind us. Our small bitch, Leenie, always attacked snakes. She would bite them on the tail several times, shaking them violently. The hapless creatures would turn around to try to retaliate but eventually would tire when she would bite them behind their heads. She was equally industrious with mongooses. Once one clung to her nose as she clung to its tail and almighty squealing ensued from both creatures. Buddhiman's wife, Bhim, was angry that we did not bring the skull back as it makes excellent anti-diarrhoea medicine. We have seen a group of mules chasing a horse's foal, trying to kill it. Monkeys are always a target for the dogs. Once, near a river, one swam a surprisingly long way under water trying to escape. They got it when it eventually came up for air on the far bank.

The 'foot' part of 'foot and mouth disease' is distressful to see. The cure is to soak the infected feet with crocodile's urine (10 rupees per bottle from the Kathmandu zoo) and molasses. We have seen a distraught bull watching over his mate's tiger-torn body.

The only fish we have come across have been in the monsoon when some have foolishly ended up in water-filled paddy fields (first cousin to the Irishman with the same name?) and those trying to climb a concrete dam on their way to spawn.

As for birds, I am always fascinated by watching long-tailed tits diving on vultures or jumping on their back and pecking them to drive them away but unhappy to see a vulture tearing the innards out of dying cattle – that is why they have featherless necks, to stop them sticking halfway. No dying or dead cattle are attacked when they lie exactly on a north–south axis. Egrets, in flocks of many hundreds or individually amongst cattle, are commonplace. I have only once seen a dozen vultures fighting hard to get at a recently decapitated sheep's head. Our dogs have been swooped on by long-tailed tits and, twice, by an aggressive fish owl.

Only once have Buddhiman and I been swept down a river in spate – and that was once too many.

As for men, some of the *jogis* on their morning food-collecting ritual talk to me. Once an Indian Army man on leave jogged passed me before turning round to come back to ask me my 'sepoy number'? I said I didn't have one and he apologised for wasting my time. Occasionally I come across a young man giving a weeping woman the rough side of his temper. I have come across a dead person twice.

When I walk up to Tiger Mountain I carry two sticks. My reply to 'Why two?' is that vehicles have four-wheel drives and I have to have a four-legged drive.

Wearing tunnel vision spectacles means I don't see 'hand signals' from a flank. I then hear a plaintive voice asking why I am walking past without speaking. I try to smooth hurt feelings. Phatic remarks pose their own problems. I have learnt what to say to the womenfolk: when they are laundering beside the road I tell them that if they had a rupee for each article washed, they'd be millionaires by now, and often I comment on how it is the women who keep the country ticking. Sometimes I say that even with twenty-five hours in a day they could never get everything done. These remarks always have a positive reaction, with a smile and a spoken agreement. Also the obvious one to shoppers: 'It is easier to spend than to earn.' That always earns me a rueful smile. People clean their teeth as they wander outside their house. Sometimes I ask the women if they know the song Mitra Sen wrote (in 1943). 'My queen-love's teeth are like cucumber seeds and her ankles like pigeons' eggs.' None have yet admitted to knowing it.

With smiles galore, laughter often and frowns seldom, the usual questions asked of me are: how old am I? How much is my pension? What do I eat? Are my teeth my own? What religion am I? Why walk? Where is 'mother'? (Meaning my wife when my questioner sees me around the same age as his father, the relationship always being as he or she would see it, never from my point of view.) How many children have I? Political points are hardly ever mentioned and when they are they usually referred to in code.

I was once shocked to see a woman binding her screaming son with a rope and tying him to the house door. I felt I had to go and ask the reason. 'To make him do his homework,' came the unexpected reply.

I have only once been asked, by a young man, to bless the girl standing next to him so that her first baby would be a son. It took me by surprise and I still don't know if what I expressed was correct. School children, including pubescent girls, routinely ask for blessings to pass exams. I was upbraided by one such when she failed her School Leaving Certificate mathematics paper and I only managed to save my face by saying that I had not blessed the person who had marked it. I was asked for a repeat blessing and was thankful to learn that on the second time she passed. Pre-selection potential recruits are another lot wanting blessings: I am cagey then and always add the proviso, 'Were I the person who chooses … but I'm not.'

Cuckoo and dove calls, blowing tunes on my walking stick, eyebrow and knee wobbling (I tell smiling mothers that children come in two types, the real smallies and the real oldies), fingers up the nose and in the ear and …

'Grandfather, you haven't been listening. Take one of your eyes out.'

… And, by sleight of hand and a popping noise made with my tongue, the mission is completed to hoots of wonderful laughter from some and a look of almost reverence from others.

Two Epiphanies

One definition of epiphany is 'the manifestation of a supernatural or divine reality' and another is 'any moment of great or sudden revelation'. I have no knowledge of an English word that modifies either of those two definitions into 'the manifestation of seldom if ever seen corporate effort that surpasses all previous similar efforts'. I am therefore happy to use 'epiphany' because, although the reality was not 'divine' as such, nor was the revelation 'sudden', both were, if not unique, matchless and almost superhuman.

The first and longer story is but a short abstract of my *A Face Like A Chicken's Backside*, published in England and Singapore, never had more than ten Gurkhas involved and the second, much shorter but equally relevant, only seventy-nine.

I

In November 1961, it was my D Company's turn to go on operations, based on Grik to start with. We were soon sent to the Thai border and found the guerilla courier route, from Thailand to Perak and Kelantan, so we now knew where to focus our attention with definite knowledge – the first for five years.

I needed to convince the most influential Temiar *penghulu* (chief), Kerinching, to help me locate which *ladangs* (Temiar aborigine settlements) guerillas would visit. Special Branch told me it was impossible but manage it I did, in a convoluted manner, by taking a sick relative, Senagit, to Grik for treatment. I brought him back, cured but weak, and hereby gained their trust. Senagit had married a girl from Kelantan where Kerinching's counterpart over the divide, Bongsu Helwood, lived.

I had made an ally of the one man who had recent connections with the chief guerilla, Ah Soo Chye. Could I get officialdom, with all its prickliness, to let me plan, then act, on whatever resulted from Kerinching allowing Senagit to go with me, with two others, his son, Sutel, and brother, Rijed? 'You will take them where you will, they will be trusted men. Only you, no one else, with a handful of soldiers can go, not to wear jungle boots [so tracks would not be seen as military] and not to have any airdrops.'

My area of operations was 1,200 square miles, neatly divided into two by the main divide. The lowest pass was 4,500ft high and, starting out at only 500ft, we had to make twelve days' rations last for forty-eight. The weight problem was such that all the men carried loads heavier than their own weight. I, weighing 132lb, carried 128lb.

I based my tactics, hence the size of my team, on three groups of three, with myself to go where I considered necessary, and all to be based on four principles: secrecy, security, surprise and simplicity.

I selected nine men and gave them a thorough briefing and told them that, were we successful, the consequence could be that a Gurkha battalion's presence near the border become a permanent requirement and that was very important as even in those days there were rumours of cuts in the Brigade of Gurkhas. I also told them that there was no compulsion for them to go on this operation; I would in no way think less of a man if he opted out. I said that all I could offer them was toil, sweat, hunger, boredom, dirt, probable failure and that I would leave any sick man behind with one man as escort. None refused to go.

The doctor had said we could exist on a diet of 5oz a day, so I decided to stick to that amount plus ½oz of tinned food (5½oz a day equals 1kg of food just short of every six and half days) from what we carried until we came across some tapioca. I could not know that we would be four weeks and 50 miles before being able to increase our daily ration or to find any tapioca.

Movement was a misery. Our hockey boots slipped on the slopes of the hills and offered no support walking in the boulder-strewn streams. Every hour we halted and took about ten leeches off each ankle. Our loads were so awkward that keeping upright was a constant challenge and the going was slow beyond belief. Every evening we drooled over our meagre rations and our loads, so teasingly containing our food, in no way seemed to lighten. Our guts knotted in hunger pains: 'self-imposed prisoner-of-war conditions', as one citation put it.

We learnt that Ah Soo Chye was not in Perak so there was only one place to go, Bongsu Helwood's *ladang* in Kelantan, on the Sungei Puian. I searched for it on the map and showed it to the soldiers. There was a stifled gasp of disbelief, if not horror, at the distance: a mountain range and 45 map miles away.

My target was about 4 miles short of Bongsu Helwood's *ladang*, on the Sungei Blaür. By now time and space meant nothing, every footstep was a challenge. Every other emotion, even hunger, was lost during the time we moved, with the terrain so difficult and our burdens so heavy and cumbersome that everything else was blotted out. We seemed to sweat from behind our eyes. The fierce joy of taking off our loads every hour was only blunted by the pangs of hunger that then assailed us.

Senagit, as guide, was wonderful. I had developed a great regard for him and we were well on the way to becoming firm friends. His knowledge of the country was invaluable as the map was inaccurate and had patches of white marked 'cloud' over where we went. We could not have made the journey without him. I was the second European he had ever seen and the first to whom he had ever spoken. As for the soldiers, I can sincerely say that during the whole operation my regard for and esteem of Gurkhas never stood higher. A challenge was there and they rose magnificently to it.

A new commanding officer (CO) ordered us back to Ipoh so all we had suffered till then was wasted. In the two days that we waited for a helicopter, Ah Soo Chye and some guerillas came within 200 yards of us and were shielded from us by Bongsu Helwood.

We were all worn out and bitterly disappointed at the final outcome. But I was extraordinarily proud of my men: no grumbling, no quarrelling, not a day's sickness, except my persistent poisonous leech bite, which I had aggravated by cauterising it with a blisteringly hot stone. We grew wan and long-haired but never relaxed or gave up. I put this down to a great sense of purpose, combined with rigid health discipline. We had been in the jungle for fifty-two days and I was a stone lighter.

The doctor examined us in detail: 'classic symptoms of starvation'. Our haemoglobin blood count was down to the level expected in a woman who had aborted, so we were given an iron tonic. Head of Special Branch wrote to the commissioner of the Royal Malayan Police asking for me again.

I picked another team, retaining only one man of the first group. We had another powerful incentive to withstand hardship: our success would have a good chance of saving at least one Gurkha battalion from being axed; the prime minister of Malaya would tell his counterpart in England that Gurkhas were essential for long-term border stability.

On 18 July 1962 I went back to Grik with my nine men. Once over the divide – another dreadful journey as it rained incessantly – our first visitors were Senagit and Sutel. Senagit was hopeful for a successful outcome of our efforts.

We hid in the jungle while the aborigines friendly to us visited us with any news of guerillas. We had no rain for the first nine days. This was unusual but it made up for it by raining daily and most nights, from 6 August to 2 September, and heavily once every twenty-four hours, with a persistent drizzle, which made drying out a problem. What little activity we could indulge in was severely hampered. The rains continued so the aborigines came less and less, partly because all movement across the Sungei Puian was dangerous and partly because even they disliked getting wet to that extent.

As the days passed, slowly, oh how slowly, with the nights even slower, a new danger made itself apparent. None of the forest had time to dry out and large branches or even whole trees would become waterlogged and no longer able to maintain their own weight. The creaking that heralded such a fall was listened to, every nerve tingling, each man hoping that there would be time to run away to safety. The rending, tearing sound followed by a sickening thud, then stunned silence when a particularly near miss was experienced, had us with our hearts in our mouths. It was far worse at night: after the tree had fallen, we would call to one another, 'Are you all right? Is anyone hurt?' Relief would flood in with a, 'We're all right, it fell just outside the camp.' On average, we heard a tree fall once every twenty-four hours.

Thus August 1962 passed. Gradually our mental horizons shrunk to our physical one: had we noticed that that frond had grown longer? That that ants' nest was less busy? That the frog was croaking at different times?

Once more we had to leave without any guerilla contact, after seventy days' effort. Back in Ipoh some of the Gurkhas asked me, 'Sahib, what have they done to you?' 'Sahib, why are they trying to kill you?' others queried amid sympathetic clucking.

I paid another visit to Special Branch and had a talk with a senior and sage Chinese. I had expected a polite thanks, maybe scarcely veiled scorn at my blundering attempts. I was not prepared to be told that they thought I still had an 80 per cent chance of success, whereas no one else was thought to have any chance at all. Despite being gratified to hear that, it seemed that I was destined for another hard slog. He had certain details: the guerillas had allegedly congratulated Helwood on keeping troops away and to the south. I had hidden more than 5,000 yards to the north and the guerillas were reported to have approached Blaür from the south-west. To me this was indicative that guerilla movement was coincidental with and not occasioned by my departure. I chose another team, new except for one man from the first time.

After an even more gruelling approach march, the area chosen for us by our Temiar guide was vile. It was full of sandflies and mosquitoes and sloped so that any sort of movement was difficult. I realised it would drive us mad to have to try to live there for any length of time, so I resolved to get the aborigines to reconnoitre another site as soon as they reappeared. We were all miserable. Bad security by others meant a new plan: I would split my force, leaving five men at the camp in ambush and move, with the other four, far south to a place called Gemala. I would first go to Blaür, meet my own company that would have flown in by then, continue south and then wheel round, having dyed my face black so not to be recognised as a European from a distance and walk back, a total of 60 miles.

All one morning I had heard helicopters shuttling in with the rest of the company only a short distance away, so I started off on the morrow, 21 November. It was the twenty-sixth day of that phase of the operation and the 148th of the series. The bad diet, the long journeys, the heavy weights had all taken a greater toll of my strength than I had realised. We only had just over a mile to go. We started off at 11 a.m. and I expected to be with the rest of my soldiers at Blaür by noon.

After about twenty minutes I realised that I was at the end of my tether. The ground had sloped gently downhill, but now it levelled out and even rose slightly. I suddenly found I could not get my right leg, which happened to be behind, in front of my left leg. I stood, legs separated, looking down at them, wondering how I could get them to move. My men waited patiently. Seconds ticked by. Nothing happened. One said, 'Come on, Sahib, let's get going,' but nothing happened. I mumbled something about trying and with a supreme effort brought my right leg forward. I looked up at the men, confident that I was all set to move because hadn't I managed to do what I was supposed to in getting my right leg forward? But I was wrong. I was still stuck. I had forgotten the simple truth that, when the right leg is in front, the left leg must be behind. I did not know what to do, nor did I greatly care. I sat down in a crumpled heap and waited half an hour for some strength to drip into my body. We were only a few hundred yards from our objective.

I was pulled to my feet and I stumbled on. I was defeated, completely and utterly, empty of any feelings, except the realisation that I was beaten, physically, mentally and operationally. All my efforts, all my high hopes, all my stubbornness, all the military stupidities I had had to fight against, all to no avail. I had lost. I stumbled on. We followed the line of the Sungei Blaür, the river that met the Puian, not so very far away. The *ladang* was at the junction of these two rivers and this was where my company HQ had established itself.

Five hours after we started I thought I saw a man washing at a ford in the river. As I looked at him he became blurred and began revolving. Then he was not there, but he was really as I could see him standing on his head. It was all very strange because he had gone when I looked again. I peered around and saw where he had gone. He had climbed some crude steps up the far bank. We had arrived. We linked arms and lurched across the water, splashing each other as we faltered. Then we were on the other side.

I only just managed to climb up the steps and there were my men whom I had last seen in Ipoh. I heard an intake of breath as they saw me. I looked at them and, for a brief moment, none moved. I swayed forward and the soldiers quickly moved to help me to a rough seat. One I had known for ten years was moved to tears as he looked at me and two others walked away so they need not see me.

I could not stand, nor sit, nor lie. I crouched forward, put my head in my hands and sobbed. Dirgaman Rai, my Gurkha captain, soothed me and ordered a man to brew some tea. Kind hands removed my pack. I wiped my eyes and sat, motionless and not quite sure what to do. I was only conscious of not having to move. I drank three mugs of tea, but I could not eat. More kind hands must have undressed me and put me on a bed made of cut branches but I never felt them. Even in my sleep angry red swirls of aches seemed ever present. I was myself again next morning: very sad, very stiff, very weak, with my walk to Gemala an utter impossibility.

We rehearsed surrounding houses in our own *ladang* at night, just in case Ah Soo Chye visited. We had cut clubs and had four teams of ourselves and Temiar. Apart from that we lived quietly in our camp until we were recalled, after eighty days, because the battalion had to go to Brunei.

I was intensely proud of the camaraderie between my three teams and me, the men's unwavering support for me ('We couldn't have done it with anyone else'), despite unsupportive battalion politics that filtered down to us and going against the wishes of two generals, one in charge of the Federation Army and the other of Gurkhas, and of Special Branch. They did this with no grumbling, no quarrelling, not a day's sickness and no giving up despite gnawing hunger, debilitating boredom, but with unwavering vigilance and ever-present efficiency. To cap it all, shining bright at the back of my mind – where it has remained ever since – was the remark passed on to me that the CO of 22 Special Air Service Regiment had told my CO that his men could not have done what my Gurkhas had done.

That was, in effect, my first epiphany.

II

The Gurkha Independent Parachute Company, to give it its full name, had its genesis in the Brunei Rebellion that started on 8 December 1962. Elements of a British battalion had to be air landed on an unreconnoitred airstrip, which was in enemy hands, something that no self-respecting air force likes to do. To clear such an obstacle is the role of parachute troops and it was the lack of them that showed up the need to have a parachute unit always on hand. Rather than denude the home base of such troops, it was decided to raise a small parachute force from theatre resources. This was provided by the Gurkhas and came into being on 1 January 1963.

Our fundamental task was to be able to capture an airhead; our next and immediate task was to operate in small patrols in advance of conventional infantry; and thirdly, we had to be ready to act as an ordinary infantry company. For our first role we had to have 128 Gurkhas, the basic minimum for all our three roles. Simple mathematics therefore meant we worked in five-man patrols, unlike the SAS, the Guards Independent Parachute Company and later the Parachute Regiment itself, who worked in four-man patrols.

Apart from being individually trained as medical orderlies, infantry pioneers, radio operators and linguists, we needed patrol training. This meant the men honing up their individual and collective infantry skills, supplemented by all the jungle lore I had acquired with the aborigines and later with the Border Scouts in Borneo, in turn built on my own personal experience gained after being jilted in 1954 when I went on twice the number of patrols than my non-commissioned officers (NCOs) to burn out my injured feelings.

In all we gave three demonstration jumps to the Gurkha recruits in the training depot in north Malaya during the brigade annual conference. I jumped first and ran over to where a public address system was ready to give the recruits a running commentary of what was happening and who was jumping. I had made a list of all those in the depot who were related to or fellow villagers of my men taking part in the demonstration. On another occasion I arranged for the Gurkha families to watch an exercise jump near Kluang. Two gores of one man's parachute tore and he approached the ground very fast. Not knowing whose dearest was so rapidly becoming whose nearest, all the Gurkha ladies hid their faces and missed most of the demonstration!

I was engrossed by a problem: our different roles demanded different types of people. One reason, so I believe, why the SAS and Para men do not always hit it off together is that the former are introverts who do not like a crowd while the latter are extroverts who do. My men had to be both. Down in GHQ the chief 'trick cyclist' had been medical officer during the war when Gurkhas were first trained for parachute duties in India, when there had been a fatality each week. I asked him his views on how to devise tests to help me chose men for such divergent tasks.

His answer intrigued me as much as my question had intrigued him: if all theatre resources were pooled and this problem was worked on for a year, he doubted a suitable answer could be found. I had to establish a personality cult, I was told, and dispense with all except pure military testing.

Before our second spell on operations we were rebadged with the Parachute Regiment badge and allowed to wear the red beret. This was much more popular than the idea of wearing our own badge, parachute and crossed kukris, as the men now felt we had been accepted by the rest of the British Army as equals.

The company made a number of cross-border operations on our next tour. Being top secret, we all had to have security clearance before being allowed to go on one. I recall opening an envelope addressed to me personally and reading the caveat stating that on no account was the person named on the reverse ever to be told that he had been positively vetted. I turned the letter over and found my own name staring at me!

In early 1966 the company returned to Malaya for a spell of retraining. I toured all Gurkha units for reinforcements and, although I only needed a modest number, I could have had 1,000, so popular had the unit become with the rank and file. With daily 'Para pay' and grade pay for medically trained men, a rifleman with me was earning the pay of a colour sergeant in a battalion. The Gurkhas were paid 4s 6d – 22 new pence – at a time when their British counterparts were getting 7s 6d, 35 new pence. The inevitable implication was that Gurkha lives were valued more cheaply than were British: I fought it hard and lost because 'Para pay' was not 'danger money' but an 'inducement to volunteer' to be a parachutist. Nevertheless, it was hardly convincing as an answer.

At noon, on 11 August 1966, confrontation ended, 'not with a bang but a whimper'. All troops in Malaysia were withdrawn from operations prior to a return to peacetime locations. We, in the Gurkha Para Company, were not in Malaysia but in Brunei, where these cease-fire orders did not apply. The Brunei government wanted to know if the last four men of a fifty-man incursion, of which my Para men had sounded the alert, had infiltrated into Brunei or died in the Sarawak jungle. In an area of wild country that could have been anything from 500 to 2,500 square miles, the odds of finding four men were infinitely remote. Nevertheless, a Gurkha patrol and a company of the Royal Brunei Malay Regiment (RBMR) were sent to the border of Brunei and Sarawak, a ridge of hilly country, to see if anything could be found.

It was by no means sure that the four wanted men were still alive and, if so, they had got anywhere near, let alone reached, Brunei. The patrol had to evacuate a man and, having nothing better to do, I flew in as the relief.

The very next day, walking along a ridge a mile or so from the Brunei–Sarawak border, I was travelling no. 4 and my eye was caught by just one leaf, lying on the ground, amongst the other thousands of millions of leaves, but it had a straight crease across it. Nature does not work in straight lines so only a man could have folded it in half. None of the security forces had been in the area for a long time so who else could it be but one of the four men we were looking for? It had rained the night before and, by then, the four men were superb at covering their tracks so the leaf was the only clue there was. The search in the area was intensified and, a few days later, a patrol of the Royal Brunei Malay Regiment captured them. During the subsequent and exhaustive interrogation carried out, it transpired that one of them was a compulsive finger twiddler, a doodler one might say, who for much of the time had a twig or a leaf in his hand. Every time a man disturbs something, the pattern of nature is broken. So that was the end of the threat of that incursion.

The original tracking work was not considered of sufficient merit to warrant any recognition as it was all reckoned to be part of the day's work. But I did especially ask the Director of Operations, by now Major General George Lea, to visit us in our camp so that he could personally congratulate the two men who first spotted suspicious marks. This he did in great style.

Back in Kluang we received news that we had been affiliated with the Parachute Regiment. I paid a short visit to England and went to Aldershot, where we exchanged presents: a ceremonial kukri to them and a statuette of a parachutist in full battle order to us. This I used as a four-monthly prize for the best soldier in the company during that period. The perks I included were to act as right marker on all ceremonial parades, to be excused all duties and fatigues, and not to have to pay any company subscriptions.

We were also tested to see if we were fit enough to become a permanent fixture in the Order of Battle. A tough exercise was thought up and we jumped from two Hercules aircraft in 'simultaneous twenties' at one-minute intervals. This was the first time in the Far East that so many British Army parachutists had ever jumped in such large 'sticks'. From the first man out of the doors of the first plane to the last man off the dropping zone was about six minutes. Not only did we defeat the enemy in less than an hour and a half – the deadline for this had been fixed at four hours – but the RAF parachute jump officer in charge, who had more than thirty years' experience, reported that he had never seen such a high standard of drop. Added to that, not one man of the eighty involved had to be put right on pre-flight or in-flight checks: the squadron leader parachute jump officer in charge and the sergeant parachute jump instructors and the dispatchers in the two aircraft told me they would not have believed such possible had they not seen it with their own eyes. This, apparently, was a brilliant 'first ever'. I was so proud of what the men had done I could hardly believe it.

That was the second albeit shorter but equally vivid epiphany I have had with my Gurkha soldiers. Both comfort me in my dotage and bolster my hopes for the future of the Brigade of Gurkhas.

On Patrol in Borneo with
an Umbrella

In January 1964, I was targeted to make a Borneo-wide survey-cum-assessment of the Border Scouts, as I was their commandant, both in Sabah and Sarawak. It resulted from a visit by a minister from England, formalised by the director of Borneo operations, Major General W.C. Walker, and agreed to by the inspector general of the Royal Malaysian Police, Dato Sir Claude Fenner. The first six weeks of my task would take me from Sabah to the Third Division of Sarawak.

After all these years, I forget who it was who told me, whilst in the Interior Residency of Sabah, to make a five-day journey into the hinterland, wearing plain clothes and unarmed, posing as a recently arrived civilian of the North Borneo Trading Company studying the *adat* (customs) of the Tagal Muruts. Fifty years later, for the life of me, I cannot believe I would have volunteered for anything so potentially unproductive. I went with two men, one a Murut himself and the other an Iban from Sarawak who had married locally.

My Gurkha gunman, Tanké Limbu, marksman and linguist, lent to me by 1/7 GR, and I started our survey from Jesselton, later known as Kota Kinabalu. Nine days later, apparently, a ceasefire was signed between Indonesia and Malaysia, after an appeal from the Secretary General of the United Nations. There was a meeting between the two sides in Bangkok. Having no radio I only heard about it after hostilities started once more.

I had been given a Borneo-wide code name, Black Prince, which was hurriedly to be changed into Brave Prince when it was realised that colour is not allowed in nicknames. It was not a name I would have chosen for myself but I felt it was better than Dirty Rat, Pin Head or some such unedifying soubriquet. Giving me the name was kind as it was thought I could get rescued more easily if I got into trouble: it was never put to the test.

We reached the local hub, Pensiangan, where I left my uniform and my rifle with a subunit of the Royal Leicestershire Regiment. I sent Tanké with a three-day recce patrol of platoon size. For my part, I changed into plain clothes – I wore thongs, a white shirt, khaki slacks and a floppy green hat – and carried a local umbrella, more as a parasol than as a parapluie. I was poled upstream by the Murut and Iban, in a *prahu*. Three hours later we reached habitation, thankfully got out of the boat and went up into a house. Native custom demands strange mouths to be fed and fed we were. By then it was about 2 p.m. and there was nothing to do until dark. The locals did not speak Malay and I did not speak Murut, so I sat on the bare floor and made faces at the children.

At dusk I was taken to another house, across the river, for the night. This was smaller and meaner than the previous one but of the same pattern: on one side of the interior were separate rooms, the remainder being a bamboo-slatted floor with, at either end, a raised portion, rather like a small stage. In the middle was a board on legs on which a continuous supply of the most grisly and putrefying fish, mud and river, and meat, monkey or pig I could not tell, on fly-blown plates, was brought by the women of the house: our evening meal. Next to the board was a bench. Between that and the board were large pottery jars, knee-high, with dragon motifs, in which was either putrefying rice or tapioca. Two bamboo 'straws' protruded through a wooden bung and water was poured into the neck of the jar on to the rotting matter inside. We menfolk took turn and turn about at sucking the circulating water through a bamboo 'straw' and at chewing the bits of smelly stuff that were small enough to come through the 'straw'. I, as guest, was invited to sit on the bench, along with the senior inmate, and have my first pick and suck. Thanks to the dim light of flickering lamps, I went through the motions without much ado. To see five locals sitting down bending forward sucking away reminded me of so many pigs with their heads in the trough.

There were also large gongs in this house and they were banged intermittently the whole night. Singing, rather touchingly in part-song style, riddle asking and quip making, dogs being incessantly clumped because they got in the way, women talking shrilly, pigs under the house squealing, chickens all round the house crowing, at various intervals children crying and shouting, all added to the bedlam. I lay to one side, some 6ft from the gongs, and went into a fitful doze, hoping they'd pack it in. They did, at about seven the next morning. All night!

We poled and paddled upstream some three to four hours next morning – me walking the difficult parts – and got to a similarly constructed, though bigger, house, after a wash. I had a meal, then a sleep. I was woken for another meal but feigned a headache. The inhabitants were just as noisy, all night, as the other house had been. By the morning I felt jaded.

The following day we walked through the jungle and up the river until we came to yet another house: thank goodness we had a quiet night, only disturbed by an old man coughing and moaning. That was our 'high-water' mark. We then returned, walking back to the boat, and spent the night in a house when either dogs barking or a baby crying took over after the gongs and singing had come to a halt.

And then it was back to Pensiangan. I found I could sublimate my feelings on such occasions like those and watch with a patience that those in my childhood would have found foreign. As for Tanké Limbu, he told me fervently that he wished never to have to experience anything similar again. He appeared to have been more frightened than I had been.

So what had I gained by my strange escapade? Those five days were like no others in my peripatetic Borneo life. But I had been part of 'there', inhaled the atmosphere, benefitted from the hospitality of the locals and could now better understand and evaluate certain problems. One man I spoke to (one of the very few who had a smattering of Malay) thought the confrontation was just a continuation of the Japanese war! Another had heard of the troubles – prices too high in the shops, he told me – but, as far as the Indonesian *Konfrontasi* was concerned where so many empire troops had been deployed to contain it, not a clue. I was probably the first European seen wandering around that part of the country since before the start of Second World War: I wonder if any others have gone back? I somehow doubt it.

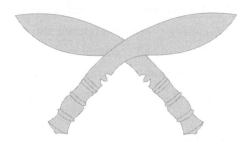

Chief Guest

In Nepal practically all functions have a 'chief guest' who has to be formally invited into the central seat on a platform in front of the expectant crowd. Living in Nepal, as I do, I find myself from time to time being asked to a function as chief guest. There are normally three types of functions to which I am invited: religious ones, Hindu and Buddhist only, never Muslim or Christian; sports tournaments; and school parents' days. I have been invited to all three, all of which require a speech to be delivered – 'now the Colonel *Saheb* will say two or four words,' is the usual formula and I heave myself off my chair, go to the daïs and start ad-libbing. I normally manage to raise some laughs. The success or otherwise of the talk is shown in the number of hands offered to be shaken by the others on the daïs on my return. However, I am practically always asked to speak at any function to which I am invited, chief guest or not.

On 14 January 2011, however, it was, for me, a first: I was asked to be chief guest in the Indian Army pension camp here in Pokhara. This time it was to start off the Nepal–India Friendship School sports day: I was warned just before dusk the day before. The invitation said the ceremony started at 10.15 a.m. on the morrow. I walked round to the camp – we can see it from our house – and arrived there a tad early. Once inside, I met a vehicle sent to fetch me and saw consternation on the driver's face. Protocol had come undone. As I was talking to the driver, the Assamese camp doctor, a major, came up with his wife. He is a delightful man and our joke is my never asking him 'How are you?' but 'How am I?'

'Get in the vehicle, please,' implored the driver. Bewildered, because I had arrived already, I did as bid and was driven about 200 yards to the CO's bungalow. The CO was Lieutenant Colonel Himanshu Bohora, 6/8 GR, whose grandfather was subedar major of 2/2 GR and was tortured to death in Singapore by the Japanese. His great-grandfather was in 2 GR and wounded in 1914 at Neuve Chapelle and his great-great-grandfather was in one of the Afghan wars.

I was bid to sit in the veranda by his wife and given a cup of coffee. I was quizzed by the colonel – what did the P. in J.P. stand for? – and then all three of us were driven back to the main Rally Ground, on which all students, from the very young to upper teens, were waiting for us, with the principal on the platform and the staff ushering the little ones, trying to get them to stand still. I was told to sit in the centre of the front row of comfortable chairs, with two cushions, and once seated there was a march past, the four houses with their coloured flags, boys in front and girls behind, giving a passable 'eyes right' as they passed us.

The colonel then rose and gave a speech in impeccable English, giving my background – that is when the P. of J.P. came in – my Indian Army service and much else. I was impressed by his knowledge. He waved a copy of *Jungle Warfare* in front of him, not that anyone could tell that my name or face were on the cover. Although he did not say so as such, anyone like myself in his mid 80s who was in India pre-partition is looked on as a rapidly disappearing member of an endangered species. In fact, for the many Indian officers who visit Pokhara, I am the first – and only ever? – such oddity they thought they would never meet.

After the CO sat down next to me and knowing I would have to speak, I asked him, 'English or Nepali?'

'English. The school's only language is English,' he replied, in a slightly shocked tone of voice.

He then left me to go to his office. An important matter had to be settled: a 7/8th Gorkha Rifles soldier, Naik Bishnu Shrestha, coming on pension, had been in a train attacked by more than forty Indian robbers. He charged them single-handed and killed three and wounded seven with his kukri, so making the others run away and getting back all the loot they dropped as they escaped. He was due to be given the highest award the Indian government can give for such an action on 26 January, Republic Day. He was also being recalled to extend his service and a lot of paperwork was entailed and, as it was a Friday, whatever had to be done needed to be done before the weekend.

The students then gave a physical training display after which 'The Colonel Sahib will now say two or four words'.

It was strange to be the chief guest at an Indian Army-sponsored function; strange to be the only non-Nepali and non-Indian there; and strange, also, to be talking in English to such an audience. I spoke slowly and distinctly, using simple words and tried not to sound like a *chi-chi*. I said how honoured I was to be there – and I meant it – and said that the mind and the body both had to be exercised. I allowed myself a short Nepali saying: 'The king never says a person is poor [enough not to pay taxes], fire never says damp wood never burns and going uphill never allows a fat person any forgiveness.' (It sounds much better in the original.) I then stood apart from the daïs so all could see me and said (in Nepali), 'I am 86. I have had the suit I am wearing for fifty years and it still fits properly. That is what I mean by keeping fit.' I was rewarded by a collective gasp from the others on the platform.

The principal then thanked me graciously and the invited guests, only a handful on a working day, went for refreshments. I spoke with the doctor, who was about to be posted. The conversation started on the impending bravery award. The doctor said he had been recommended for a bravery award but 'doctors don't earn them' had been the answer.

49

I told him that two of the three VC and Bar winners were doctors. He showed his surprise.

Somehow we then switched to discussing the first field marshal, Sam Manekshaw, and the second field marshal, Cariappa. I told him that I had not met the first one but that, at Ootacamund in December 1971, during the Indo-Pakistani War, I had been summoned to the house of the Maharaja of Porbandar to meet him.

The day before, newly arrived in Ootacamund, I had tried to find accommodation. At the first port of call two Indian ladies from South Africa were holding forth at the reception desk about the colour bar. I, as the only European in a bunch of Dravidians, was eyed suspiciously. 'Tell me, mister,' importuned one of the ladies in her sing-song accent, 'where is colour bar?' I looked at her, wondering how best not to become involved. 'I know where is this Malabar,' I countered, 'but I am not knowing where is this colour bar.' I left abruptly with my baggage, seeking other accommodation, before my audience could further react.

This I found at the Savoy Hotel, a European-owned and -run institution twenty-five years out of date but still surviving. The manageress still spoke of Home, read her English newspapers disdainfully, took tea exactly at half past four every afternoon in her office (knees rug-draped to ward off the cold as fuel was so expensive) and fed her fat and pampered Pekinese pet dog on paper-thin jam sandwiches while it was sitting in her lap.

That first afternoon I called in at the Nilgiri Library. It was a fascinating place. Except for a few recent daily papers, it was a monument to 1947; nothing had changed, so it seemed. I was allowed into a smaller room, where the *Encycolpædia Britannica* (1929 edition) was kept. Here, sternly staring from a frame on the opposite wall, was a painting of the Queen Empress, presented to the library on the occasion of her Golden Jubilee in 1887. All else was much older. Dust was the only post-independence addition to the old magazines and periodicals: *Nineteenth Century* from 1878, *Frazers Magazine* from 1864, with *Bailey's* and *Badminton* equally old. Tantalisingly, *Blackwoods* started with volume 2, dated 1817, and continued intact until 1915. What ripple of the Great War lapped into that bleak room, putting an end to a ninety-eight-year collection?

I saw what I thought was a man's name, Neil Gherey, but I learnt it was the old Anglo-Indian spelling of Nilgiri, the 'Blue Hills'. I was also told that Ootacamund was the bastardised version of the local aboriginal Toda *Otha-ka-mand*, the Village of the One Big Stone. Victorians spoke of the place as 'Snooty Ooty'.

My musings were interrupted by the secretary introducing himself – an ex-major, Son Dutt. Urbane, with impeccable English and friendly, here indeed was a living link with the past. More links were made manifest when, next evening, I was called to the telephone by a staccato and dictatorial voice (which failed to identify itself) asking me my business and inviting me to breakfast on the morrow with the Maharaja of Porbandar. The latter then came to the telephone when the invitation was repeated and, mystery settled, General Cariappa would also be there. It was the general who had heard from Major Son Dutt that a British Army officer was in Ooty. The general, the first commander-in-chief after the British left India, had retired some years before. He was in Ooty giving a lecture to the Indian Union Club Cultural Centre on 'Mother India'.

Breakfast the next morning was good. The general and I had fruit, porridge and cream, rumble-tumble, followed by toast, butter and the Maharani's home-made marmalade. However, it was fasting day for the Maharaja, who nibbled a raw carrot, and for the Maharani, who toyed with a banana. The general monopolised the conversation. He suggested to the Maharani, who was the secretary of the Indian Union Club Cultural Centre, that I give them a talk. I demurred, pleading a clash of dates. The proposed lecture was then brought forward to a Thursday (the first time in our club's history) and I was obliged to name my subject. I chose 'South-East Asia – Historic and Prophetic'. Thus it was that many little notices appeared all over Ooty during the next few days, advertising this supposed attraction.

Soon after this the party dispersed. The general drove down into the Plains, escorted for the first few miles by the Maharaja and Maharani, who showed him a short cut through the town. There farewells were said. I accompanied the general some distance in his car before returning to Ooty by a previously ordered taxi. 'What wonderful English the Maharani speaks,' I ventured. 'Should do,' he said. 'She's a Welsh woman.' I learnt that the Maharaja had captained the first Indian Test XI to England in 1932 as well as being an international squash player, an author, an artist and a composer. Talented and positive, the ex-ruler was one of the Old School.

That bit is for the reader's background. In Pokhara I turned to the doctor and said, 'Doctor sahib, you will be the only serving officer in the Indian Army who will know what I am about to tell you about Field Marshal Cariappa. On our way down into the plains, the general, not a field marshal then, opened up. He, a stickler for time, told me how he had once thought he was late for the function to which he was driving himself:

Just as I came to a level crossing the barrier was dropped. Passage barred. I called the gatekeeper over and said to him in the local language, 'Please lift the barrier. The train won't be here for five minutes. Please let me through.'

'No,' came the answer, so I waited impatiently. As soon as the barrier was lifted, I sped through and, 5 miles farther on, the same thing happened. The barrier to another level crossing came down just as I arrived. Again I pleaded in the local language but the answer was the same. I glanced at my watch. I was worried. When the train had passed up went the barrier and through I dashed. Colonel sahib, you will not believe me when I tell you a few miles farther on another barrier came down just as I arrived.

This time I called out to the keeper in English: 'Open the bar, you bloody fool. What the devil do you think you're doing?' and open it he did. I slipped through and arrived just in time. *That's* the way to get around …

One has to have discipline. My daughter was married to a captain. That first evening, after the party, I told the new bridegroom, 'Breakfast is at eight o'clock. Be punctual.' He came down at twenty past. I was angry. I said, 'after breakfast you will go back to your battalion and have a week's extra Orderly Officer and only then can you go on your honeymoon.'

By this time the doctor's, the other guests and the assembled ladies' eyes were button bright.

'And another point I'd like you to know – and I guarantee no one in the Indian Army knows this,' I continued, bit between the teeth. 'In 1936 or 1937, at Alexandra Post, on the North-West Frontier and at 8,200ft high, the highest fortified position in India, Captain Cariappa handed over to Captain Vaughan, the first CO of the British Army 1/7 GR. Vaughan [the men pronounced his name "Bhagwan"] told Cariappa to open a sealed box of 2in mortar ammunition. Cariappa cavilled: "It is sealed," he said. "You have signed for a full box of 2in mortar ammunition."

'"I want to count them," said Vaughan, so he opened it and, horror of horrors, it was full of sand. A court-martial offence if ever there was one, especially on the Frontier.'

The excitement of my listeners was obvious.

'The paperwork made its way to the highest authority. Everybody expected a court-martial but, to everybody's amazement, nothing happened.'

'Why not?' asked the doctor.

'Because,' I said, 'even as long before independence as that, British officers knew that the post-independence army would need good officers. It was obviously a mistake and he was given the benefit of the doubt.'

And heads shook in wonder, smiles appeared on all faces as a different view of pre-independence British India found appreciation.

Time to leave. I said my farewells and, although prepared to walk back, I was taken by vehicle.

All in all, it was a different ending to an unusual chief guest day.

I wrote both to the principal of the school and the colonel on the morrow. In the latter's letter I put that I had missed the Indian Independence Medal by two minutes. My disappointment had now been fully obviated by such a wonderful and happy occasion. And why not?

Aimed or Unaimed?

If you would hit the mark, you must aim a little above it.

'Elegiac Verse' (1880) Henry Wadsworth Longfellow

Sixty-two years later I can still see it happening, nor have I finally made up my mind whether the woman acted deliberately or not – she never looked behind her before, during or after her short squat … and yet? But first things first.

My A Company, 1/7 Gurkha Rifles (GR), was stationed in Rompin, in the Bahau District of Negri Sembilan, Malaya. Our camp was contiguous with the larger part of a Mr Smith's main estate. His nerves were still stretched overtightly from having been a Japanese prisoner of war. Several miles away to the north, close to the jungle, was a small offshoot of the main estate, run by the sub-manager, a Geoffrey Fermin,

In those days, early 1952, guerilla re-supply was often managed by rubber tappers taking food with them to the remoter tasking areas near the jungle edge where it was handed over to them. Fermin told me of a three-day period when and where this was likely to happen. I said I'd be there, with my men, from soon after dawn on the morrow.

(I must break the thread of my story briefly: since 2001 I have lectured all new recruits, Brigade of Gurkhas and Gurkha Contingent, Singapore Police. One point I stress is that the small, seldom, if ever, recorded incidents, properly carried out and normally taken for granted, are the hallmark of Gurkhas being superior to most, if not all, other troops and which have helped give us such a high name. In fact, the continuous dedication to such matters is the obverse of the coin of collecting bravery awards and without which the coin would be valueless.)

We moved out of the camp on foot, lay up till dawn and made an approach march through the jungle and, half an hour after dawn, deployed on the edge of the rubber estate on a small mound overlooking a laterite road, a stream and a latex-collecting shed. We camouflaged ourselves as best we could and lay prone in the cover crop, at best not more than 9in high.

For an hour nothing happened.

Inexplicably, because Fermin had told me he would not come our way, I then heard voices and saw Smith, with a shotgun and a large black Alsatian dog, and Fermin, walking down the road towards us. Behind them by several yards was their Malay Special Constable armed escort. They stopped just short of the stream.

'John Cross and his Gurkhas are in ambush positions just in front of us,' the garrulous Fermin said.

Smith was outraged. 'What? Without asking my permission. How dare he?' He raised his shotgun to his shoulder and pointed it in our direction. 'If I see him I'll fire at him and kill him. If I don't our escort will.'

He turned to his dog and, gesticulating in our direction, sent him searching for us. The dog ran down the small slope, jumped over the stream and started sniffing its way up towards us.

I 'froze' more stiffly than before, in the unhappy realisation I could do nothing else.

At the same time, a Chinese tapper woman had been coming our way, flitting from tree to tree and deftly cutting the bark so letting the latex drip into the little bowls that had been hung lower down the trunk.

She had to be aware of the Europeans and their escort. I saw her tuck her cutting implement under her belt and start walking backwards towards the nearest soldier. As she went she lifted her upper garment, undid the cord of her trousers and, squatting almost on top of the soldier, pulled her knickers down and pissed.

I saw that we could come to grief even before the dog had reached us: I shuddered and inwardly squirmed at this totally unexpected addition to our possible discovery – two pairs of European eyes, many more of the escort, a searching dog and now …

Finished, she stood up, arranged her clothing and moved off to the next tree to continue her task. Simultaneously, the dog, only yards away from us, turned and went back to his master.

'You're wrong, Fermin,' I heard Smith say, sneeringly. 'My dog would have found anyone there.'

I did not catch Fermin's reply.

By then it was obvious that no guerillas would be coming that day. After the two men, the escort and the dog were well out of sight, I lifted the ambush.

'How did you manage not to let her know you were there?' I asked the soldier.

He had watched her come towards him and, as she squatted, was amazed to see something never viewed from that perspective before. 'I'd have been wetted if I hadn't moved my head, just in time.'

Had her stream hit the soldier more than a penny's worth, in panic, pot shots and a possible post-mortem, would have been spent.

Back in camp I rang Fermin, who had told me that Smith's visit up to his sector of the estate had been a surprise, and relayed his conversation back to him.

'Will you tell Mr Smith?'

'It hadn't occurred to me but I will.'

So I did. 'Geoff Fermin told me you and he went to the edge of your northern estate this morning.

'Yes. He told me you were there. Had you been I'd have shot and killed you.'

'But I was ...' and I started quoting him and his deputy word for word, of course including the 'kill him' bit. I heard him breathing heavily into the mouthpiece, even more heavily when I came to the tapper woman bit.

Initially, he was stutteringly speechless at what I told him. 'If you hadn't relayed my conversation back to me I would not have believed you,' he stammered eventually. 'I can't think of any other soldiers who could have hidden as you did.'

'Neither can I.'

Nor can the twelve intakes of Gurkha recruits' Queen's Gurkha Officers (QGO), warrant officers (WO) and non-commissioned officers (NCO) who have also heard the story.

Cross Words

When working in the Centre for Nepal and Asian Studies, my second and last of two projects was seeing how much Nepali had changed since Professor Turner produced his dictionary in 1930 and the production of a compact Nepali dictionary in 1983. For twenty-one months I read through Turner's Nepali dictionary twice and, at the end, felt like that Scottish lady who had done precisely the same with an English language dictionary, apparently thinking it was a novel. She said that she 'found the plot verra interesting but a wee bit concentrated'. The same person is also reputed to have read the Edinburgh telephone directory through from cover to cover and her comment then was also 'verra interesting' but that there were 'too many characters in the plot'.

Why, any rational person might ask, did I read through Turner twice? I was comparing the definitions he gave with those in the Nepali– Nepali dictionary, produced by the Royal Nepal Academy in 1984 as a Tribhuvan University linguistic project, with a view to seeing how the language had changed during the last sixty or so years. I admit that it was hard and, at times, boring work and I also admit that the immediate practical use of my findings fits neatly in with the British Army's definition of a hovercraft – 'a solution looking for a problem'.

Apart from my work being of possible use to linguists, scholars and examiners, it could well be of considerable value as the basis of an updated version of Turner: the Great Man, in a letter to me, wrote, 'I feel I must encourage you to proceed with your intention of producing a new dictionary … which will fill many of the gaps in my own.' Alas, even with such encouragement as that, obstacles for production of such a work are many, varied and expensive.

A certain American called Ambrose Bierce defined a dictionary as 'a malevolent literary device for cramping the style of a language'. That was around the turn of the century and, having been immersed in words for so long myself, I feel he has a point. When faced with the challenge of comparing any shifts in meaning and spelling in sixty years of Nepali, I felt that there might be a few hundred and that I could go out 'into the sticks' and see what sort of Nepali was spoken by whom and where any differences were to be found. However, I had not been prepared to find that a minimum of 15,760 of Turner's 26,000 headwords did not agree with the Nepali–Nepali dictionary and that, with an average of three entries for each headword, a staggering total of 47,280 differences emerge.

The Nepalese are very fond of riddles and I wondered out loud to members of the Linguistic Society of Nepal how they would answer this one: what is it we use most of but give least thought? There were no prizes for guessing the answer: words. We use them when talking, reading, writing, singing, thinking and dreaming. We use them more than we use lungfuls of air in any twenty-four-hour period. Wars are started with them and battles are lost because of them; money is made or lost with them; almost every one of our actions is affected by them; we hear them poured out at us in an unstoppable torrent, often with scant regard as to their real value – on and on and on – until we become satiated with them, don't listen to them properly or just ignore them.

Some people find mastering languages hard, while others find it relatively easy. Those who find languages hard generally find mathematics easy. The nearest to mathematics a language can get is legal language when every word should have only one strict interpretation. This is when the aphorism of the famous short-story writer H.H. Munro ('Saki') – 'A little inaccuracy sometimes saves a ton of explanation' – breaks down.

It is estimated that English has a million words, three-quarters of which are technical. That leaves 250,000 'ordinary' words. The *Concise Oxford Dictionary* has 74,000 entries and language pundits have it that the range of vocabulary of a well-educated adult is between 20,000 and 30,000 words. So what about the other 200,000 to 230,000? Within every language can be found words that mean different things to different people, words that can seem innocent of any broader meaning and words that seem to mean nothing at all! In the first category, 'I'm mad about my flat' can mean either 'I'm very angry about my puncture' or 'I'm very pleased about my apartment' depending on which side of the Atlantic one is brought up or dragged up. I don't have to emphasise what people would think if they heard 'I feel a perfect ass' when spoken in the dark, unless they could tell it was British English!

Nowadays, even the use of the once eminently respectable words has to be careful, otherwise the user is liable to be drummed out of the Brownies, as the meanings and connotations of certain words have changed over time. Also, if words have not exactly changed their meanings, misuse of them causes false impressions. For instance, 'decimate' means 'to kill one in ten' and not 'to leave only one alive in ten'; 'disinterested' means being 'impartially interested' and not 'uninterested' and 'verbal' means 'using words, either spoken or written' as opposed to signs. But still 'verbal orders' and not 'oral orders'!

As regards the second of my three categories, the elliptically rendered sentence 'I felt it was all up with me; I had been working all out and was now all in, so it was as good as all over', is only a slight exaggeration and could also have been written, 'I had been working hard and was now exhausted, so all was finished'. As for phrases that seem not to mean anything at all, apart from 'the car broke down as the school broke up', how about 'now then, come on, let's go'?

If you were to ask anybody if they spoke their mother tongue, you would be told not to ask stupid questions. But, however well a person knows even their own language, it fails to give exact descriptions of, say, a picture, a pattern or even what happens the moment a bullet leaves a weapon – hence the expression 'a picture is worth a thousand words'.

The apt choice of words used plays an obvious part in understanding fully what is meant. 'Did you see the dog's tail in the moonlight?' and 'did you observe the canine appendage in the lunar effulgence?' can be seen to mean alike, but what about the civil servant who saw a memo and thought it such nonsense that he felt obliged to pencil 'round objects' beside the offending part? Months later, having been circulated in all the many offices, the same memo came back with the puzzled query, 'Who is Mr Round and to what does he object?' You can't win them all!!

As I see it, there are three types of English, or of any language come to that – normal conversation, prose and poetry. Few people are capable of sustaining 'spoken prose' for very long and anything written in the vein of conversational language often fails to 'come across'. English conversation suffers from such defects as false starts, changes of structure during speech, hesitation, repetition, pauses and other distortions, where most Nepalese seldom have to correct themselves, limiting their verbal tics to '*kere*' (and what) or '*chahine*' (one sort) rather than the many such in English – 'yer know', 'sort of', 'I mean' and, on occasions, 'between the jigs and the reels' or 'in a following wind'.

In the framework of comparative analysis, trying to decide which dictionary was 'correct' was beyond me. Certainly I could say that, as far as hill men are concerned, words in Turner seem still to hold sway over some modern versions but, and it is a very big but, who is to be arbiter in the majority of such changes?

As mentioned earlier, there are at least 47,280 of the wretched things for consideration. On the other hand, I have to admit that I learnt something new every day (some senior officers say this is 'a good thing'), which however unlikely it seemed at the time, may stand me in good stead one day. I had already learnt that *jangal* (jungle) originally meant 'a place bereft of trees' but I was frankly ignorant on how ganglions affected yoga; the invisible rings round the navel; which lunar mansions are auspicious and when; and the twenty-one individual hells of Hinduism. Trying to unravel these esoteric meanings meant resorting to a Sanskrit–English dictionary where again I found the going hard. How to choose between 'raven', 'snake', 'boar', 'potter', and 'hell'? And 'colour', 'redness', 'love', 'joy', 'anger', 'song', and 'musical harmony'? To say nothing of 'white', 'black', and 'the third fold of skin of an elephant's left buttock'. How indeed? I waded dutifully through all these and many others until, thoroughly bemused, recalled a pundit of 1/7 GR, the late Bhimlal Sharma, telling me that he had studied Sanskrit for only nineteen years, so was still not well versed in it – and finally understood that he was not exaggerating.

Incidentally, after the opening of communications between Pakistan and China, a small community living in an utterly remote area was found to speak a language the nearest ever heard to Sanskrit. It provided a field day for interested linguists who had thought that such a phenomenon had died out more than 2,000 years ago. One meaning of *Sanskrit* is 'purified' and *devanagari* means 'god of the city', so highly was literacy rated in very olden times. Today, Sanskrit is regarded with religious veneration. I have only every heard of one other instance of linguistic deification, so to speak, and that concerns Thoth, the Egyptian god of definitions, worshipped in 2000 BC. However, if one really wanted the ultimate in useless linguistic knowledge, I cannot do better than tell you that the Vietnamese for Dharan (eastern Nepal) is Dien Bien Phu, with the 'Dien' bit being no more than 'district of …'

Some derivations of Nepali words reflect the French presence in India, with *kamij/chemise* and *patlun/pantelon* obvious instances of this. An example of English influence is *Kampani paisa* after 'John Company', the most used Nepali name for Indian currency until recently and it is still known by that name in the hills, while *chultho* – a bun of hair – was the name of the 4-anna bit (*chulté paisa*) more than a century after

Queen Victoria's effigy in that hairstyle disappeared from the 1*d* coin of her early reign. Nepali words such as *gulab* (rose) and *sabun* (soap) seem to appear in most languages between the Gulf and the Yellow Sea, as do traces of many other words, as exemplified in the one example of 'brain' – *MOKaj* and *diMAGH* in Nepali and Hindi; in Thai and Lao *saMONG* (with different tones); in Vietnamese *ÚK;* and the Malayalam for 'with no brain' is *aMOK*, ergo the English 'amok'.

It has been said that in Nepali, used at village level, it is hard to express concepts or abstracts. This aspect of the language, extrapolated into Gurkhas speaking English, is patent when technicians are on advanced courses in Britain. With the spread of literacy an earlier defect has been remedied to a great extent.

The imaginative use of language is evident, though, at proverbial and onomatopoeic levels, and the one I like best is the description a muleteer gave when his mule was kicking and bucking like a wild thing, which it was: 'The mule ran away, high jumping and long jumping.' On the other hand, vagueness can defy every apt translation with sentences such as *ita uti gardai lañdai malai kaso kaso lagera tyatikai bhai gayo* – 'it passed over after a bit of upset'? I don't know; as the bishop was once overheard saying to the actress, 'context is all'.

One of the interesting (to me, at any rate) aspects of playing with words is seeing how Grimm's Law works between one language and another. This – when any consonant changes only within its group but vowels can vary – is a commonplace among many European languages but not so obvious or common between Nepali and English. Three spring to mind: *mantri* and 'minister'; *kendra* and 'centre'; and *dubida* and 'doubt'. This also seems to operate sometimes between Cantonese and English, for example: *tok* (poison) and 'toxic'; or 'learning'/'reading', *tuk* (Cantonese), root *doc* (Greek) in 'doctrine' and 'doctor'; *yan* (Cantonese singular) *man* (Cantonese plural) for English 'man' and Nepali *manchhe/ manis* (intriguingly a Hindi/Nepali word for 'man', *admi*, also means 'descended from Adam'); and *ma* (Cantonese for 'horse') gives English 'mare' – female horse – and 'a man who leads his men from horseback',

a 'marshal'. 'Talking on the telephone' in Cantonese is 'fighting with
the electric speech', or *ta tin wa*.

As I sat one evening on the side of a path near the village of Barang
in Dhading district, I was fascinated to see a rare dance of one Nepalese
ethnic group. A group of men approached me. They were emulating
spear-waving foot soldiers, in dress and gait, and were escorting their
commander who, not in step with his band of men, was also dressed
in martial style and had a small horse's head tied in front of him and
a horse's tail behind, showing him stylistically mounted as 'fighter on
horseback' or, as we now all know them, *ta-mangs*. They sang as they
passed me – haunting yet urgent. Whether it was a paean of victory or
a dirge of defeat, I could not tell, nor even if their song was of happy
or cross words.

My Sapper Grandson's Wedding

The most important family occasion of the year 2014 was indubitably the marriage of Buddhiman and Bhimkumari's elder son, Sapper John Pahalman Gurung, in July, to Rita Gurung. He had fallen in love with his future wife using a, to me, new-fangled gizmo, Facebook: he in the UK, she in Kathmandu. Not that it had anything to do with it but I had enlisted the bride's father thirty-six years earlier – too far back to be incestuous. The date of the wedding had to be the most auspicious day for the zodiacal match and, if the two could not be united on the earliest day for auspicious matching, 2 July 2014, there would not be another for about three and a half years. So the groom had, somehow, to get to Nepal (from Edinburgh where he was on a piping course) for the day and luckily a three-week break in the course allowed him to come to Nepal.

Getting the invitation cards out was a major operation in its own right; there were so many people to be invited. In some cases they were given out traditionally, using betel nut, not paper. I gave out 'distant' ones on my morning walks, Buddhiman the nearer ones. He is well known over quite a large area; indeed, he has had his photograph on the left-hand side of the masthead of the most widely read English-language newspaper. He is the man in charge of all traditional songs and dances for Lamjung district, as well as for much of the area around Pokhara. We have been the longest in this area, twenty-eight years, and were the first house here – fear of a leprosarium had kept folk away. Also, being the surrogate son of a British Army lieutenant colonel, a large invitation list was expected. In fact, although more than 3,000 invitations were given out, there were still about 1,000 people who felt they should have been invited. When tackled by such malcontents I say that, as second best, I'll invite them to my 100th birthday party.

Furnishing arrangements for the bridal bedroom, spring-cleaning of house and garden, including repainting of gate and outside walls and catering arrangements – out to contract – took a lot of time. On 25 June, three days after my sapper grandson got home, we had to go to Kathmandu, where the bride-to-be lived, for the official engagement ceremony. 'We' meant the extended family, travelling in a minibus and a car. We left on the 125-mile journey at 6.30 a.m. but it took us till after noon to get to the girl's parents' house as blockages on the last uphill part of the journey slowed us down. Five gallons of home-brewed country spirit, in specially marked jars, one goat and 254 pieces of flatbread were offered to the in-laws-to-be, to say nothing of five new suits for Buddhiman's other son and nephews (and 255 new *saris* for all female extended family members, of whom only daughters and some nieces travelled) and wedding rings and gold ornaments for the engaged couple. After offerings were made and the engagement made official by the exchange of finger rings, we had speeches and a meal, following which we came back again, reaching our house at 11 p.m.: a long day for me.

On 2 July an even more extended family travelled in two larger buses and a car, with the back window suitably decorated with a 'J', a heart and an 'R'. First we had a religious ceremony in the house and our own temple: the groom dressed in red and silver traditional Nepalese fig with a white turban. We all had to give him a religious rice *tika* on his forehead before he left the house – his cousin, Sombahadur, walking behind him, covering him with a traditionally open umbrella. There was a three-hour hold-up on the way to Kathmandu so everything was delayed. I (thankfully) did not go.

Heavy monsoon rain blighted everywhere on the day before and day after but the day of the feast itself was dry and hot. For the reception in Pokhara, I wore a Nepalese fig and a waistcoat, as some sort of 'over-dressing' is obligatory with that form of dress. After their late arrival in Kathmandu the actual marriage took place, after which whatever else had to be done was done and then the main meal, due at noon, was taken at 8 p.m. – after being reheated several times. Even then they could have got back to Pokhara by 5 a.m. but there were two more three-hour stoppages (minibus accidents). They got back at noon, more than three hours after the first guests turned up. The return journey had taken twelve and a half hours, yet no grumbling. Fate!

Guests had started to arrive at 9 a.m. so Bhimkumari, daughters and I helped feed them with customary tidbits and a meal – the catering was done by contractors, with fifteen goats being slaughtered *on* site, but not *in* sight. The 250kg of chicken meat, 225kg of fish and 200kg of sausages were brought uncooked – the cooking being done on the premises. The bride, groom and a few others did not reach the house by car: they had got out in the local market, about ¾ mile away, where the bride, veiled, was placed on the back of an elder brother. The groom, still escorted by Sombahadur and shielded by that open umbrella, along with Buddhiman, walked in the hot sun to the house, then around the house – the veil-covered bride on her brother's back all the while. There was much excitement on the road and more on arrival; I, tunnel-visioned, kept out of it for fear of bumping into people. As the new bride entered the house, she had to tread on five small wicks that had been put into small mud 'pies' and put the flame out with her feet.

Later on bride and groom sat together on throne-shaped chairs near our household temple and guests gave them rice *tikas* and traditional silken scarves. Several hours later the pair were allowed to disappear for a break for, by that time, they were tired. Meanwhile, there were three lots of dancing (the local ladies had danced till 3 a.m. outside the house the night before) with three lots of different types of noise. The last guest arrived at 8 p.m. and the last meal was finished at 11 p.m. In all, probably more than 3,000 guests arrived: 2,160 bottles of beer, 84 bottles of whisky and 360 containers of soft drink were drunk and 400 cigarettes puffed. Buddhiman had sold some land at a good profit so the final bill was, in effect, halved – but it still had to be paid!

And still, on the morrow, the women once more sang and danced till the afternoon when all those many, many who had helped with the arrangements were traditionally thanked by Buddhiman (and me), until dusk. But even that was not all: a couple or so days later the groom, on his way back from leave, plus his parents and the new bride had to go to Kathmandu and spend a night in the bride's parents' house and, a week later, the bride's parents and a couple of family members drove down from Kathmandu to do the same with us. In the latter case, time was against them so they only stayed a few hours before driving off, having been fed and watered. Still, a most protracted performance indeed.

Cure or Curse?

In the spring of 1943, towards the end of *Bikram Sambat* (official calendar of Nepal) 1999, young Janga Bahadur Gurung of Nalma in Lamjung married a girl from the smaller village of Naské, two hills away to the east. The ceremony was as countless others had been over the centuries, with *lamas* presiding over the actual details: what was different, although certainly not unique, was that boy and girl had fallen in love with each other at first sight. She was still young, in her early teens, so, as custom dictated, she returned for a while to Naské. One of the guests was Janga Bahadur's friend, Debi Bahadur from Kabre, a small village on the east of the River Midam, just a two-hour fast walk away.

Before the end of the marriage season Debi Bahadur also married – with Janga Bahadur, his guest – but of love there was none. Debi was the poorer and could not afford such a lavish ceremony so paid his band of musicians a smaller amount than had Janga paid his, or so it was understood. The Nalma band let it be known they had received much more and this caused jealousy and, had anyone been there to see it, a bizarre performance took place on the first Tuesday of the Nepalese New Year, 2000 BS, when the band from Debi's marriage assembled by a *chautara*, the stone edifice built for weary loads of gossiping villagers to rest on. There they waited until a gust of wind shook a dried leaf from either the *bar* or the *pipal* tree that were always planted side by side on the *chautara*. The seven men watched the leaves fluttering and, as a leaf dropped, they tried to place themselves underneath it and catch it in their mouths. If they were successful, it signified a curse had been put on the instruments of the other, the Nalma band. A record of five leaves were caught.

After Dashera 1943 the two lads went to India to join the army. They were seen off from each other's houses with the age-old ritual of the eldest woman of the house feeding them both with milk from a vessel that she held in her hands, two leaves of the sal tree being wrapped around the container so she did not touch it. They then had a white cloth tied around their heads. Later, inside the house as they sat cross-legged near the open fireplace, two other women bound a narrow strand of saffron ribbon round their necks while they said, '*Sya sya sya*'; all the other members of the household pressed the youths' heads while the ribbon was tied. The two lads were then part of the other's household.

A few weeks later they were enlisted. They both went to the same regiment up in the Himalayan foothills, 1st Gurkha Rifles, at Dharamsala. After training they were drafted away to an active battalion, leaving the Regimental Centre early one morning, on their 60-mile journey to Pathankot. The Quarter Guard turned out, presenting arms, as each platoon gave the eyes right with each man ludicrously stern in his golden youth. They marched with as much of a swagger as they could with their big pack, basic pouches and rifle all weighing them down.

Once outside the immediate confines of the centre they broke into song:

At the top of the *sal* tree the leaves are green,
We're on our way, we're on our way to the war.

Then another song started:

> Even with gold and money proffered, all in vain,
> The happy days of carefree youth will ne'er be seen again.

They were carefree. Life was full of excitement with so much that was new and romantic, heroic and challenging, free and easy. Easy? Well, hardly. One of the platoon commanders, a grizzled jemadar who was returning to his active battalion after recuperating from a wound, knew better. Also, the omens were not good. It was not raining as they left the centre; some would suffer. He heard talking in the ranks and, turning, saw it was Janga Bahadur. With a name that meant 'Brave War' he should be all right but one never knew. Jang was talking to his friend Debi Bahadur: strange name to give a man, 'Brave Goddess'. The jemadar shrugged his shoulders and shouted at them to hold their tongues. They marched on down the road ...

Both survived the war, which was uncomfortable, dreary and dangerous. They both longed to return to the cooler, crisper air of the hills after the steamy atmosphere of the Burmese jungles. They had fought in a number of battles and, as bad luck would have it, back in their villages it was rumoured that both were dead. Letters with red thread in the left hand corner of the envelope and written on red paper had reached their homes. So, despite there being no official news, ceremonial mourning took place before the two men returned and when eventually they did get back, although alive in body and spirit, they were dead as far as tradition and orthodox thinking would have it.

In Janga Bahadur's case he was stopped outside the village bounds, halfway up the hill, and was allowed no farther. That evening blankets and food were smuggled out of the village for him and the elders sat in council pondering on the magnitude of their problem: a dead man alive but his wife a widow. Eventually a solution was thought out: he would have to be reborn. Accordingly a hole in the earth was dug and Janga Bahadur was entombed therein for ten days – the hole being the womb of Mother Earth and each day representing one month of confinement according to lunar calculations. Every night food was smuggled out to him – smuggled because being unborn he could not eat, so needed no food.

The ceremonies of birth, including cutting the cord, through to taking his first solid food six months later, were telescoped into six days when the band was assembled to play at the weaning ceremony. It was then that the curse of the Kabre men worked; three drums split and two wind instruments broke. Consternation reigned and hurried consultations took place. The omens had to be divined and then the horrible truth dawned: remarriage between the two could never be formalised as, although Jang had been reborn, the gods would have taken it as incest.

Jang was ordered out of the village. That night he was joined by his wife and, as soon as they could the next morning, they left the area never to return. At the time of writing (1982), they may still be alive: in their state they have been classified as belonging to the Kiranté Bangsa, devotees of the god Mahadeu, or so the older Brahmans of thereabouts will still tell you, so someone, somewhere may have had mercy on them.

As for Debi Bahadur, he knew he was dead as a man although he was alive, so he came to the conclusion that the only way he could reconcile this situation was by wearing women's clothing, thus appeasing the 'goddess' he had been named after. His wife had already gone with another and after the horrors of war and the confusion of mind resulting from his traumatic return he became slightly disturbed. Being unwilling to stay in his home area any longer, he went to India and lived, where he had once trained, near the River Ghaté. In Kabre he is still remembered as 'Ghaté Khola Saiñli'.

As Others See Us

O wad some Pow'r the giftie gie us
To see oursels as others see us!
'To a Louse', Robert Burns (1786)

I

On pages 448–50 in his magisterial book *Defeat into Victory*, Field Marshal Sir William Slim has written a detailed encomium about a minor incident that took place in February 1945 involving one Sherman tank and two platoons of 1/7 Gurkha Rifles against some Japanese. These latter were 30 yards in front of the attackers as they dashed for safety towards their previously prepared bunkers. The Gurkhas, advancing in bounds supported by tank fire firing solid shot into the bunkers, killed and captured them with bullets and bayonets. In his narrative Field Marshal Slim pleaded some indulgence for the length of the description for three reasons: that it was the nearest he had been to the fighting since he had been an army commander; that it was one of the neatest, more workmanlike bits of infantry and armoured minor tactics he had ever seen; and that he was colonel of the regiment of the attacking Gurkhas.

One of the section commanders was Naik Lalbahadur Limbu, a strong, thickset man with a robust sense of leadership and more brawn than brain. Seventeen years later, Captain (QGO) Lalbahadur Limbu, DCM, MM, was second-in-command of D Company. I was his company commander. He had the greatest respect of his men but, by then, had a strained look on his face for much of the time and seldom smiled. The battalion had been on Malayan emergency operations for longer than any other Gurkha battalion, 1948–59, without a break. And the following two years in peacetime Hong Kong – the first time the battalion had had proper accommodation since the end of the Second World War – had made life towards the end of Lalbahadur Limbu's soldiering a much more complex and complicated affair than even he had been used to. Under peacetime conditions his company clerk and platoon commanders 'carried' him as much as I did. In 1961 we moved to Ipoh, in north Malaya, and at long last the old man's service came to an end.

We gave him a farewell party. He declined when I first asked him to address us, I having made my speech about him and his service by then. He had never been particularly good at speaking, relying on gestures and blunt grunts more than on detailed descriptions. I invited him once more to speak and he accepted. What he said has stayed with me ever since, more than sixty years later as I write this, as it struck a cord with its simplicity and truth. He started off bluntly and surprisingly: 'You British are strange people. You give a soldier a reward and for the rest of his service you give him a reward for having given him a reward. Let me tell you what I mean ...

'Towards the end of the Burma War I chased and bayoneted a few Japanese soldiers. The army commander sahib was watching and gave me a Military Medal [MM]. That was fine. I had never asked for a bravery award but if the Sarkar [the government] wanted to give that to me of course I would accept it.

'In 1947 we had "inding-pinding" [Indian independence] and our 1/7 GR was chosen for the British Army. I was called into the company office and the major sahib asked me if I wanted to go with the battalion to Malaya or be transferred to the Indian Army, or go back home? "I have to warn you," he said, "that as you are not very clever you will never be promoted higher than *naik* but, as you have an MM, you'll be welcome in the battalion. What is your choice?"

'I told him that I had never asked to go higher than *naik* so was quite satisfied to go with the battalion to Malaya.

'Once we got to Malaya our A, B, C and D Companies changed to P, Q and R Batteries as we were made into artillery. After a year that was cancelled and we went back to normal. I was called into the company office and the major sahib said, "Corporal Lalbahadur, now we have four rifle companies, we are a sergeant short. You will be promoted to sergeant but I have to warn you that you will never be promoted higher than that. But you have an MM so sergeant you will be but you'll never be promoted any higher. Have you anything to say?"

'I told him that I had never asked to go higher than corporal but if he wanted me to be a sergeant, sergeant I would be.

'I was then sent north with a couple of platoons where we were ambushed by a crowd of *daku* ["*dacoits*", the word used to describe the Malayan communist terrorists [CT]] and, after an hour's battle we killed some and drove the others off.

'Some time later I was awarded the Distinguished Conduct Medal [DCM] and, after the investiture by the high commissioner sahib in Kuala Lumpur, I was called into the company office by the major sahib and told I was to be promoted to warrant officer, Class 2, company sergeant major. "You have a DCM so you'll manage but you'll never be promoted any higher. Have you anything to say?"

'A few years later I was sent for by the commanding sahib. I was marched into his office and told that, as I had a DCM and an MM, he was going to promote me to lieutenant [QGO]. "You'll never get promoted any higher. Have you anything to say?"

'I told him that I had never asked to go higher than WO2 but if he wanted me to be a lieutenant then lieutenant I would be.

'And just before the battalion went to Hong Kong the new commanding sahib called me into the office and told me he was promoting me to be captain and here I am, going on pension as a captain. You British are strange people: I was rewarded twice for what I was enlisted as a soldier to do and all my promotions came as a reward for already having been given a reward.'

And he shook his head almost in disbelief as he sat down to rapturous applause.

And of course the opposite can happen. It is seldom indeed that a soldier or officer, having been punished for one mistake – however noble his service, however good he was on operations, however much his men would follow him wherever he led them – would be promoted any further: the antithesis of Lalbahadur's litany, a punishment for having been punished.

The case I quote refers to another soldier in my A Company, Tulbahadur Rai, with whom I was privileged to serve with, first as a sergeant when he was awarded the DCM and a mention in despatches (MiD). Later, when in charge of the Demonstration Troops at the Jungle Warfare School, he was put up for a British Empire Medal that eventually became a Commander-in-Chief's Certificate.

There was only one other QGO in the battalion who may even have been fractionally more skilled in the jungle than he, one Sudaman Rai, of C Company, I believe, whose nickname among the men was *jangali kira*.

Tulbahadur's story is modestly told in pages 190–6 in *Gurkhas at War* but, having been out with him on most of the occasions we contacted *daku*, I know that much of his personal prowess and bravery was understated. I commanded A Company from the end of 1952 to mid

1956 and during that time we had thirteen confirmed kills and two unconfirmed, along with four captures and, apart from that one DCM, two soldiers were awarded an MM and eight MiDs. That may not sound like many successes but one statistic I worked out was that the enemy was in a rifleman's sights for around twenty seconds in 1 million man hours (about 800 man years) during security force operations. All in all, we didn't do so badly.

I never operated with Tulbahadur again and, after the battalion's two years in Hong Kong from 1959 to 1961, I spent much of the next year on Operation Bamboo, south of the Malay–Thai border. The rest of my eighteen years' service was spent elsewhere. I learnt that Tulbahadur had been made Gurkha major but, along with many others, had offended against the stringent law of smuggling gold back into Nepal. (This was a widespread practice despite the penalties for being caught: unproven rumour had it that more attempts were successful than not.) For that he had been punished for a truncation of his period as Gurkha major and not been awarded any honorary rank.

I happened to be in England, half blind, with Buddhiman, my surrogate son and my eyes, when the Duke of Edinburgh, piloting his own helicopter, landed in Church Crookham to take the salute on a rainy day, for, I believe, the last time the battalion officially paraded. I learnt that all past Gurkha majors had been invited to attend. I looked around for my old comrade-in-arms and, not seeing him, asked why he was not there.

'Not invited,' I was told. 'The only one not invited.'

'But why?' I queried.

'Caught smuggling.'

'But he was punished for that, surely, and still remained a Gurkha major?'

But no invitation had been given because of that one mistake. Having been punished once, he was punished yet again despite all those wonderful and dedicated years on operations that brought fame and renown to the battalion.

In Sarawak I once met a Royal Marine brigadier who proudly told me, over a 'cup of wet', that he had been put on an adverse report when a major, taken his punishment and soldiered on. 'I never thought I'd rise this high,' he said with a smile, 'but,' he added, not as a dig I like to think, 'in the Royal Marines we are only punished once for anything we do wrong.'

I forget my spoken answer but I thought sadly of Tulbahadur – a Gurkha, not a Marine.

II

As Others See Others

Researching for a rewrite of *Jungle Warfare* (2008), I came across a number of books that had not been published when I wrote the first edition (1989). In sum I learnt that, in the Burma War, the Japanese considered British troops indolent, effete and outdated, and Indians and Gurkhas cowardly and disloyal.

Most Gurkhas said that African troops were careless and noisy, and did not put sentries out during periods of rest or take other precautions. Others saw them as clumsy and cruel. One man, Lance Naik Indrabahadur Rai, 1/7 GR, told me that he had seen African soldiers eating Japanese flesh.

Gurkhas' views on Japanese bravery were rightly circumspect, knowing the Japanese 'mental inoculation' against worrying about death. 'Only when we knew that we had no hope of staying alive and were virtually dead already did we know that we could beat them properly,' was the tenor of remarks made to me. However, on Japanese ethics, Gurkhas' views were wholly negative: Lance Naik Indrabahadur Rai came across 16 Casualty Station where he saw all the ambulances thrown upside down, some in water, and that the British doctors had been crucified on trees. He and his friends rescued them and Indrabahadur said that they all eventually recovered. From then on, all Japanese were devils. Another Gurkha saw six men hanging crucified from trees. 'The Japanese are trained to be cruel,' he told me.

Another Gurkha, Lance Naik Makansing Gurung, 3/4 GR, was adamant that 'the Japanese lost the war although they were better trained and better equipped and cleverer soldiers than we were. They lost because they were small-minded and greedy. They are very sinful people.'

The only live Japanese soldier I came across in Burma was on a patrol with B Company, 1/1 GR. The man was lying on the ground on the western side of the Pegu Yomas, unable to walk. I had been issued with a book that showed English questions on the left of the left-hand page, with the Japanese equivalent on the right-hand side, and possible answers, in two similar columns, on the right-hand page. He scared me by asserting that there were many thousands of troops in the direction a patrol had gone – I hoped that nothing untoward would overtake the Gurkhas. In the event it transpired that he thought I had asked him for his army number! So engrossed was I that I did not notice that he was drawing his pistol to use against me but a quick-eyed rifleman prevented him from inflicting any damage.

Background to Brahmanism
in Nepal

BRÂHMAN: (neuter) 1. The Supreme Being, regarded as impersonal and divested of all quality and action; (according to the Vedântins, Brâhman is both the efficient and the material cause of the visible universe, the all-pervading soul and spirit of the universe, the essence from which all created things are produced and into which they are absorbed); 2. A hymn of praise; 3. A sacred text; 4. The Vedas; 5. The sacred and mystical syllable om; 6. The priestly or Brâmanical class (collectively); 7. The power or energy of a Brâhman; 8. Religious penance or austerities; 9. Celibacy, chastity; 10. Final emancipation or beatitude; 11. Theology; 12. Brâmanical portion of the Veda; 13. Wealth; (masculine) 1. The Supreme Being, the Creator, the first deity of the sacred Hindu Trinity, to whom is entrusted the work of creating the world; 2. A Brâhman; 3. A devout man; 4. One of the four Ritvijas or priests employed at a Soma sacrifice; 5. One conversant with sacred knowledge; 6. The sun; 7. Intellect; 8. An epithet of the seven Prajâpatis; 9. An epithet of Brihaspati; 10. An epithet of Siva.

V.S. Apte, *The Student's Sanskrit-English Dictionary*, 1890

Although Hinduism is the major state religion of Nepal, Brahmanism – that is to say the way the Hindu upper crust treat that religion and other Hindus – is a state of mind. *The Economist* newspaper, in its Christmas 1982 edition, wrote: 'Man is by nature a religious animal … and it matters because he is also a particularist, tribal, intolerant and aggressive animal.' It is no good wearing Western Christian spectacles to try to understand Eastern Hindu Brahmans, the type of person most frequently met in Nepal.

Two basic and fundamental differences of belief in, perception of and relationships between Hinduism and Christianity shape, colour and influence to a lesser or greater degree all the thoughts and actions of believers of both faiths, consciously or otherwise, throughout their lives. In essence, Hindus will say 'I am God' whereas Christians will say 'I and God': for the former it matters who you are, not what you do; for the latter it matters what you do, not who you are. All other religious and cultural differences stem from these two. A Hindu's religion is influenced by two facets: *karma*, the position into which one is born, the points one has to score for the next world and any aspects of a past life that have to be paid for in this incarnation; *dharma*, acts, functions and observances that have to be followed to ensure enhancement. My own definition of religion under such circumstances is 'behaviour focused on salvation'.

On the surface the many similarities, not diversities, between such people and those from amongst the humbler Hindus may mask degrees of emphasis rather than basic differences. Brahmans find it difficult to come to a decision and abhor confrontational situations. This leads to grey areas of accommodations rather than the black and white of absolutes. This encourages there being no sense of accountability, no public conscience, no ethical censorship and, outside the family, no moral imperatives. This, in turn, leads to what is known as *indrajal*, a 'web of deception', which makes that which a Western Christian would see as a straightforward and simple matter, Byzantine and convoluted in the extreme. This affects standards of comparable probity to the extent that undue intransigence, lying and false witness are apt to be a defence against hostile consequences of too hasty a resolution of a problem. This is this approach used by functionaries, including the police, who thereby put themselves above the law as we, not they, see it. Maybe a parallel in the Western world would be looked on as unsavoury political opportunism. However, as far as Nepal is concerned, unless there is a signed and authenticated piece of paper as proof, does a person say what he means and mean what he says? Probably not: it is not prudent always to be stark in speech and much, in Nepal, is said by leaving so much unsaid, with hint, inference and gesture carrying much weight.

How is it that this state of affairs came about? A look at the past might help cast some light on that which is, to many, inexplicable.

Mythology and religion are inextricably mixed on the subcontinent. The home of both Hinduism and Buddhism, India's religious influence has long penetrated other parts of Asia, while ideas alien to both philosophies have been absorbed within its culture. The Vedic philosophy of unreality, *maya*, the illusion that considers the unreal universe as really existent and as distinct from the Supreme Spirit, has also spread to Buddhism (Maya was the Buddha's mother). This basic philosophy has not always sat easily with extraneous religions, and tensions still arising from Islam and Sikhism show up all too clearly from time to time. As for the earlier phenomenon of Christianity, the original Coptic Christians who arrived in India in the fourth century were accepted by Brahmans as equals. Since Abbé du Bois' proselytising foray in southern India for a quarter of a century from 1789, Brahmans have put Christians below the lowest of Hindus, calling them *Mlechchha*.

If Buddhism could more easily cater for the needs of the traveller in the very early days by satisfying his religious instincts while not having to be tied to a particular location in order to carry out all that the religion ordained, Hinduism, by contrast, was essentially static, inward-looking and self-centred. The core beliefs of Hinduism are much more easily grasped by Christians than that which has emerged over the centuries and is practised today.

A Roman Catholic priest, wearing the saffron robe of a Buddhist monk and adhering to the code of conduct laid down by the Enlightened One, will not be unfrocked or excommunicated: the same does not apply if he embraces Hinduism.

The Hindu caste, or colour, system is based on the Vedic theory of the divine origin of the caste system, which makes a change of status impossible. This has fostered the belief in reincarnation to a higher caste, for which religious rituals and generous gifts are prerequisites. The legal authority for the 'divine right of caste rules' is found in the most aged and venerated Hindu law book, *Manusmṛti*, upon which the Nepalese legal code is ultimately based. It is essentially male-oriented and with a political rigidity not unlike the bishop-clergy-laity syndrome that kept the early Christian church intact. Fear of the unknown, unquantifiable and assertive elements of a fanciful cosmic world was so strong that basic survival needs could be given a religious, therefore a not-to-be-questioned, authority. Had cattle in those very early days been slaughtered to extinction, milk products, pullers of ploughs, leather and manure would not have been enough for basic needs. Today, certain swathes of forest in Nepal are preserved only by a religiously inspired fear: even to pick firewood is to invite divine retribution in the form of hail to flatten the crops. No ugly landslide scars that disfigure so many deforested hills elsewhere mar these protected areas. Similarly, in the harsh, arid, dusty, hot world where Islam took root, control of rabies and intestinal worms would have been impossible had dogs and pigs not been placed under religious discrimination. That which attempts to sanctify marriage for Christians is also given a spiritual authority to try to make that contract binding.

King Prithvi Narayan Shah founded modern Nepal in AD 1768. It was he who said never to trust the English but always be polite to them; it was he who said that as long as there were Indian merchants in Kathmandu there would be tensions; it was he who expelled the six Italian Capuchin monks who were then proselytising in Kathmandu; and it was he who declared that Nepal was the true 'Hindu-stan'. This last has been perpetuated in the constitution of Nepal, which proudly announces that the country is the only Hindu state in the world, with its royal ruler seen as semi-divine. During the century of Rana rule, many of the excesses of Hindu practices were modified or discouraged, especially by Maharaja Jang Bahadur. Aspects of child marriage, divorce for women (whose status, regrettably, sometimes still borders on that of a chattel) and modified rules for committing *suttee* are examples.

Hindu cosmology divides time into four ages, each fostering a progressive decline in morality, piety, strength, happiness and longevity. The present, and final age (due to expire on 18 February AD 428,898), is supposed to be the age of promiscuity, both sexual and religious. However, according to modern Hindu reckoning, the world is even now at the end of the Age of Deception and is about to return to the first one of all, the Age of Truth, as people become more unruly, tensions increase due to lawlessness and conflicts escalate, until the world is destroyed by fire and flood. The description in the *Ramayana*, written between 1200 and 900 BC, could apply to the cataclysm following the detonation of a few nuclear warheads and polar ice caps melting to inundate the Earth.

The pantheon of a myriad Hindu gods and goddesses sees all aspects of man's nature, good and bad, portrayed on a cosmic scale. Love and hate, sincerity and treachery, good deeds and sinful actions are all aspects of the gods' own behaviour, which can uplift mankind or bedevil it with destructive relentlessness. If the whim of the gods manifests itself adversely and callously by an individual not having paid due attention to making all the necessary oblations and sacrifices – however trite and trivial these may be – it is the fault of the individual. Placating, warding off wrath and spite, and acting as a god's slave are constants: those whom the gods have made their heirs, the twice-born Brahmans, view those below them as the gods view mankind – an attitude that feeds on bigotry.

There is a continuous juxtaposition between all aspects of malevolence and benevolence, manifested by the ancient Hindu symbols of, for instance, a male and female swastika and the two triangles (*shatkon* or six angles, also a male and female unity) that the world knows better, but incorrectly, as the Star of David. Never really knowing which side of the coin may be revealed and with an eye to the main chance, toadying, flattering, fawning and a subservient approach to one's masters, therefore, ward off calamities more effectively than, say, do accountability or any moral imperative. This is still found in the ancient and time-honoured system of *chakari*, for which a dictionary will give only a vapid and shallow translation of 'service', 'domestic service', 'duty' or 'attendance'. Sure, but much more also: it includes the calculated acts of servitude, generally menial, designed to reward the doer with worldly advantage. *Chakari* apart, three English words are used to describe avenues of self-betterment: 'force' or money, 'source' or personal contact and, a poor third, 'course' or qualifications.

A corollary to *chakari* is the 'crab culture'. A crab will see another crab climbing up a slope and will fasten itself on to a limb, thus preventing the climber from going any higher: if an advantage can be accrued by stopping another's advancement, it will be taken with, best of all, the stopper making use of what the stopped might have made use of. Conversely, any advancement at another's expense should be made in inverse ratio to it, not merely as a simple progression above it. This is not seen as unfair, nor do personal relationships normally enter into the equation.

The primordial urges of status, fame, power and prestige are found everywhere but only Brahmans have the four birth-given rights: religion, worldly goods, sex and salvation, in that order. All need to be satisfied. In brief, religion means the retention of Hinduism with its caste structure and observances, although these were modified in law by the late King Mahendra who decreed around thirty years ago that all Nepalese were equal; worldly goods account for the constant itch in pocket, purse and palm and an eye to the main chance wherever gain is possible. The criminal law that allows all crime to be compounded by its monetary value, thereby allowing the guilty to 'buy' himself out rather than serve time, reinforces this desire for wealth. This could be the root of the Nepalese proverb that roughly translates into 'greed to gain to ruin'. These two concepts tend to clash as *Manusmṛti* (2:168) discourages economically productive work for high-caste people. For them to be competitive and aspiring to better themselves run against their religious grain. Interestingly, religious programmes on Radio Nepal are completely dominated by values of self-negation and emphasis of spiritual values. Sermons hold out no promise or hope for the poor and deprived except in the life hereafter.

Sex is an endemic religious attribute, as shown with these two examples: the epic poetry of such hedonistic amorous frolics as performed by Krishna and the cow girls and 'wanton sporting with other maidens' (*Gita Govinda* by Jayadeva, written in the twelfth century); and the Tantric erotica found on temples. In society it translates into a man's inherent right to more than one marriage to beget sons and not to die a widower even if it means an 80-year-old marrying one scarcely a teenager, while salvation allows cosmic forgiveness for any mondial failings.

Fatalism, induced and imbued by centuries of a rigid society riveted to unfathomable whims and unshakable prejudices, is unbelievably strong. The power that the gods have over a person's life is 'written' on the inside of the forehead. None can see it till after the head has become a dried skull and even then none can read it nor understand it. Unchangeable, inescapable, omnipotent, it, not its owner, is responsible for successes and failures in life. This should induce modesty for the former and does induce an attitude of non-responsibility for the latter.

The division of humanity into four castes and thirty-six colours, as laid down in *Manusmṛti*, was only introduced into the valley of Nepal by King Jayasthiti Malla in AD 1382, after the Muslim invasion of November 1349, when most sacred Hindu shrines were effaced, if not destroyed. These divisions soon spread and are still widely observed throughout the kingdom. They are seen by some outsiders as a more odious and insidious form of apartheid than any practised elsewhere, yet no Brahman will take that view, even though some Brahmans will say that these divisions were not found in core Hinduism but were applied by Aryan conquerors of India (from modern Iran (= Aryan) and Eastern Europe) as a form of maintenance of racial superiority. They are enforced by the four fundamental 'rights' that give an absolution as potent and complete as any propitiatory sacrifice. Conscience is not inconvenienced. For Christians to call Hindus *Saitan* merely exacerbates the situation by diminishing the dignity of the former and increasing the intransigence of the latter.

Personal relationships and families – nuclear, extended and *mit* (non-blood relationships of binding attachment) – are of the greatest importance, but within their own framework. There is no security outside the family circle, which is unpredictable and malleable. In families, loyalties, priorities, ties and obligations dominate behaviour on a scale unknown in many parts of the world. As for personal relationships, a Nepalese proverb tells of 'an ox-selling relationship'. No matter how far back, any previous satisfactory transaction by a member of one family with a member of another stands other members of both families in good stead. Until a personal relationship exists, virtually no interest is exhibited or even wanted. A stranger slipping on a banana skin is regarded as a jape of the gods to relieve the watcher's boredom. Strange dogs sniff one another cautiously: Brahman strangers will endeavour to establish a link as a priority before anything else, whether for business, a free meal or a helping hand. Once any link has been forged it is normally binding for life.

For centuries Westerners were not allowed to visit Nepal and this isolation still affects many Nepalese perspectives. It was only after 1950, after the country started to be opened up, that the need to define distinct national values – including political philosophy, dress and language – was felt because of Nepal's desire to keep aloof from what was seen as Indian political hegemony. Confrontational tactics are rare in Nepal, where pressure applied from behind the scenes is preferable. The declaration of a Hindu state in the constitution compelled the policy makers to define these values in relation to Hindu ideas and primarily high-caste Hindu values. Time also has its own value; it is either auspicious or not. If the former, all that has to be accomplished within its appointed limits must be achieved for success, no matter the inconvenience; if the latter, then it is not important, nor need it be adhered to under normal conditions of, say, routine appointments. It is not looked on as money. One point of good Nepalese manners that foreigners do not instantly recognise as such is that it is wrong ever to appear in a hurry or that there is work to be done.

Brahmans' view of their language and writing differs from Christians': *Sanskrit* (meaning 'purified') has the echo of the gods still vibrant in its every cadence, so must remain in its sacred form, even to the tenor of the voice when reciting or praying. Writing has sacred connotations as *Devanagri*, the name of the script used both in Sanskrit and modified slightly for Nepali, means 'god of the city'. Around the same time (2000 BC) the Egyptians gave Thoth the status of 'god of definitions'.

Despite all natural inclinations to remain separate, Nepal has become more prone to Indian influence as communications, tourism, business interests, education, films and the Indian population within the country all grow apace while, in India, despite it being a secular state, the main thrust of governmental values has mostly been in the hands of high-caste Hindus, so replacing with their values those associated with the Raj or northern European Protestants. These latter included civic duty and honesty in public life as the bedrock of colonial faith and now also embrace devotion to charitable affairs and a caring welfare state.

During these last thirty years, certain Nepalese cultural changes have been observed, caused, in part, by a much greater general awareness of the outside world. For Brahmans, changes noted include: fewer people wearing the sacred thread; the discontinuation of the raised platform on which the ritually dedicated cooking place for twice-born eaters would be placed; cooking by non-twice-born unmarried daughters; the discontinuation both of certain religious ceremonies and recitation of sacred mantras; eating poultry, eggs, tomatoes, onions, white sugar and factory-made biscuits; drinking liquor; and not changing into a *dhoti* before eating. Elderly Brahmans are caught between that which is understood, the traditionally ritual and hierarchic, and a yet-to-be-understood secular approach to life.

Ethnic societies in Nepal are labyrinthine and abound in intricate complexities that defy easy comprehension. More and more, as Nepal develops, do modern and ancient, industrial and agrarian, religious and secular vie for retention and acceptance without there being enough room for them all. Unified, yet diverse, influenced over the years by the Cold War between the communist giants in Asia, an India that wants to be undisputed regional champion, the third world, the do-gooders and the evil-doers, measuring progress is not easy. G.K. Chesterton's aphorism, 'progress is simply a comparison of which we have not settled the superlative', is especially relevant in Nepal's case.

It is only since the early 1950s that Nepal has opened up and foreign organisations have set up agencies and sent people into the hinterland. Unspoken or not, unhappy comparisons are made constantly between the financial backing and efficiency of foreign organisations and any homegrown equivalent. A covert function of anything foreign is sadly and almost always incorrectly seen by a large percentage of Brahmans as Christians trying to undermine their god-given position of supremacy in society and simultaneously fostering the enhancement of non-Brahmans. Nothing seems to convince them otherwise. Brahmans are indifferent to the goodwill, as opposed to the efficacy, behind foreign organisations which are not seen as an instrument for good (some Brahmans objecting to that which Mother Theresa has done not so much as affecting a person's god-given karma but more as a threat to the old and established order), never forgetting that Nepal is the only Hindu kingdom in the world and one that has never been any country's colony, despite it having had to pay tribute to the Chinese during its history.

The degree of empathy between Indian and Nepalese Brahmans may sometimes manifest itself more strongly than purely national ties would be expected and normally dictate. What many Nepalese do not seem to realise is that, were it not for the Ranas and the British, Nepal would have been an Indian colony long since. Some Brahmans seem to wish that to be the case now and it is this factor that, in the election of 1991, the Communist Party of Nepal vehemently, and probably successfully, accused the Nepali Congress Party of having as policy.

A Brahman's religious views and priorities affect his conception both of politics and of the civil administration, so all three are apt to become entwined. Many Brahmans, taking their cue from India, were not happy with the *Panchayat raj* system and its political philosophy as partyless could be equated with 'classlessness'. Such people see foreign aid as the main prop that kept the present constitution in place: replace the prop and change is bound to eventuate. Anything that was thought to prop up the regime was seen by these people as being inimical to their interests. To make matters worse, foreign organisations are seen as being activated by Hinduism's enemy, Christianity, which is portrayed as an English colonial weapon – indeed I have been asked where in Britain are Jerusalem and Bethlehem. Although the Congress government has promised that Christians will have freedom of religion, it was still too early to read the tea leaves of any Hindu backlash. Even so, it is surprising how many there are of this faith, albeit many such can now only be classified as 'closet Christians'. Sadly, despite this, religion is in danger of being polarised as, almost as if to balance that promise, the 1990 Hindu World Congress that met in Kathmandu stated that Nepal must remain a true 'Hindu-stan'. With *Ram Raj* resurging as a political reality in Indian politics at the same time, the effects of *Manusmṛti* will be reinforced.

That having been said, a constant conundrum and peculiar paradox of the 1991 election, the 1980 referendum and the first attempt at a multi-party democracy from 1951–62 is the addiction so many Brahmans have shown to communism. This could be a facet of 'a dualism so contrasting as to suggest a schism in the soul' of Brahmanism: the philosophy that incorporates both the 'rarefied monistic spiritualism of the *vedanta* and 'the materialism of the less-known *charvaka*', where virtue is a delusion. Be that as it may, the attraction of communism in Nepal has been in inverse ratio to its demise in the rest of the world. Canny communists are telling people that religion and communism are compatible: another case of that dangerous mixture of the plausible and the gullible. Communism is asking again all those questions that the Hindu world deemed answered forever, as well as some of which it may never have considered. In Hindu Nepal many who see the smile of the communist sphinx misconceive its meaning. The paradox of Brahmans espousing the cause of communism, when the rest of the world is repudiating it or basing itself on the Indian Congress party when not even its most dedicated supporter could claim more than a modest success in some areas in forty-five years of independence, could be a combination of a genuine desire for a Nepalese solution to late twentieth-century Nepalese problems. This is compounded by the Hindu inability for both original thinking and making decisions. The nearest they can get to their prescribed remedy for modern ills are those remedies to problems that had no Nepalese content in their origin.

Those who have read *Manusmṛti* will see that the king's position in the country has been weakened now he has been placed within the constitution. With the hierarchical status of the monarchy subsumed by the state, similar treatment of their hierocratic aspect in Nepalese society will seriously weaken the position of the Brahmans. Their reaction may not be good news for Nepalese Christians.

Another factor in the equation is that there is much Indian influence in Nepalese school textbooks (the 'Bible and sword' syndrome) and from certain unscrupulous political circles in India. This has found an incredulous audience among school children. Purveyors of such influence also try to make out that the Nepalese monarchy gets its strength more from foreign sources than from Nepalese subjects. Royal visits to foreign institutions, therefore, enhance and encourage this absurd belief. (The monarchy was abolished in 2008 and Nepal is neither a Hindu kingdom nor state.)

The appearance of foreigners in Nepal is believed by some to be responsible for the spread of Christianity by internal osmosis often spurred by a desire to escape life under the tyranny of Brahmanism. In fact, the most ardent proselytisation has been practised by Nepalese and Indian Christians. One effect of this has been the polarisation of both the Hindu and Buddhist religions. The Middle Ages' triptych of Christians, Turks and Infidels has been replaced, in modern Nepal, by Hindus, communists and Christians.

The sadness of the Brahmans is that they can believe no truth that does not paint the world in their colours. Thus it is that any such facet as Western/Christian welfare (in its broadest concept), which uses a colour base that is foreign to Brahmanical thought, makes it an alien graft.

It is difficult, as well as rash, to 'stand up and be counted' when talking about the future – except to say it is bound to come. Vague mutterings of regional 'explosion', 'implosion' and 'absorption' can be heard. Even though doom is not on the doorstep, an awareness does exist of there being no return to the static rigidness of the past. All realise that the pace of change has never been quicker. Many Hindus are asking themselves if this means a hastening of the end of the present Age of Deception and a quick return to the primordial purity of the Age of Truth – and, if so, can this be achieved without the expected holocaust?

Those of us who are guests in this country need to exercise patience, tact, wisdom and understanding so that the Nepalese may gain from our presence, and not end being the losers.

Faith in his British Officer

Deserved but Dashed

I never knew his name but, when I first wrote about him, I named him Himan Dura, aka Lothé. His nickname means 'imperturbable'. I worked out that he lived between 1921 and 1945; in 1939 he enlisted in 2/1 Gurkha Rifles. He was held as a prisoner of war by the Japanese and somehow managed to escape from Singapore but he never volunteered to be part of the turncoat Indian National Army (INA), also known as Japanese Inspired Forces (JIF, sometimes known even as Japanese Inspired Fifth Columnists). I was in the 1st Gurkha Rifles Regimental Centre in Dharamsala at the time of his amazing arrival and managed to pick up his story. The adjutant, fifty years later, became a close friend of mine. Charles Wylie, mentioned below, was also a great friend of mine in later years.

Early January 1945, Dharamsala

Snow lay thick on the ground, up to the roofs of the bungalows in the cantonment area. By the time Lothé had reached as far as his railway warrant took him, Pathankot, reaction had set in. He had just enough money for a bus to take him to Lower Dharamsala and he had to walk the rest of the way to the camp. Not far but almost too far. By the time he reached the camp he was on his last legs. He remembered where the office block was. He pushed his way forward, intent as never before, to honour his inner resolve to do what Wylie sahib, the adjutant of 2/1 GR, had told him to do, all those many moons, nay years, before – 'try to get back and tell them what happened'

Men called to him, seeing a stranger, albeit a Gurkha stranger. He took no notice. He walked round the parade ground and staggered up the wooden steps that led on to the verandah where the offices were. The stick orderly tried to stop him. Lothé ignored him; his automatic compulsion, his overriding urge, drove him forward. He pushed open the door of the adjutant's office.

Sitting at his desk the adjutant acted angrily at this unwarranted interruption and without even a knock on the door. 'What the …?'

He was interrupted. 'Hajur. Rifleman Himan Dura, 2/1 Gurkha Rifles, reporting,' announced Lothé with as smart a salute as he could manage. The regimental number he gave was indistinct and the adjutant did not pick it up.

'2/1 Gurkha Rifles, did you say?' stuttered the gasping adjutant.

Lothé opened his mouth to reply but crashed on to the floor in a dead faint: physical decrepitude but not moral turpitude the cause.

Only a week later did the doctor allow the adjutant, Captain A.P. Coleman, to visit Lothé. 'Are you ready for me to talk to you?'

'Sahib, that is why I have come back,' answered Lothé, smiling broadly.

'Right. Here I have the battalion long roll. We will go through it together and, as far as possible, you will tell me what has happened to people.'

'Sahib, I can only tell you exactly who was dead, who was missing, who was wounded up to the time that Captain Wylie sahib was captured.'

'I am sure that will be of the greatest help.'

Name for name, almost without any hesitation, the answer was given.

At the end of the session the adjutant was amazed at Lothé's knowledge. 'That is amazing. How can you remember all that in so much detail?'

'Sahib. I was Wylie sahib's batman. Whenever we had news of casualties, he amended his own nominal roll and, helping him to do so, I knew what had happened to whom.'

Captain Coleman shook his head in disbelief. 'And at the end, what did Wylie sahib say to you?'

'Sahib, his words were "Try to get back and tell them what happened." That is why I have come back.'

'But however have you, one man, managed when no one else has?'

'Sahib, excuse me. I am tired. Can we talk tomorrow?'

'Of course. I'll come back at the same time,' said Coleman and left.

On the morrow Lothé started telling the adjutant, accompanied by a shorthand clerk, about the behaviour of the INA, or JIFs, especially Captain, later Major General, Mohan Singh and what he and Captain Wylie had seen at the Siam–Malay border when he met, and went off with, a Japanese officer. Coleman was appalled and muttered under his breath about 'Desi turncoats'. Not only that, Lothé told of the hectoring tone used by Mohan Singh when he tried to get the Gurkhas to enlist in his INA, Azad Hind Fauj, and about when a man, who had refused to volunteer for the INA, had the full night soil bucket poured over him to make him do so. He passed out and later was not allowed to wash till he did volunteer. This he never did (and I personally interviewed him in 1999 – see *Gurkhas at War*, p. 40), and how three other men were killed in cold blood because they, too, did not volunteer. Coleman probed further and found out who was responsible for exactly what atrocities, where, when and against whom. Lothé also told him about Japanese behaviour as he related his adventures, although he had no knowledge of Japanese names.

'Although the war has yet to finish, so many of the INA have been captured and brought to India that their trials are being planned for later on in the year. Your evidence, especially about Mohan Singh [the soi-disant commander], will be crucial. No doubt about that whatsoever.'

'Sahib. I need to go back on leave but I will stay until I have given my evidence.'

The commandant, Colonel N.M. Macleod, had been sent a sensitive letter that revealed that those who joined the INA were to be graded into three categories: white, grey and black. In brief, 'whites' were those who stayed loyal to their oath, obeyed, perforce, orders given to them by the INA but did not volunteer for service with it. 'Greys' were those who, while entitled to some measure of sympathy and understanding because of the pressure they had undergone, nevertheless showed by their manner that they were suspected of actually joining the INA. Some of those would be allowed to rejoin their units. 'Blacks' were those whose conduct left no doubt that they had to be tried by court martial.

'Lothé, I have one question for you,' said Coleman, one corner of his under lip caught up on a tooth at the end as, having read that letter, a tiny, nagging doubt had occurred to him. 'Did you at any time tell the Indians you volunteered for work in Siam?'

'Sahib. Never, never, never after that night soil. I told the subedar major sahib and he did not want me to go but I then told him what Wylie sahib told me and he agreed. He personally told the Japanese in charge of our lot. Indians had nothing to do with my going at all.' Lothé was as adamant as any Gurkha Coleman had seen.

'Good. In that case your evidence will be of the greatest importance. You have done more for the battalion and the regiment than was ever expected of you. Wylie sahib, no, we don't yet know if he is dead or alive, but he would be more than exceptionally proud of you.'

Lothé looked as pleased as he felt. Before he left for Delhi he had an interview with the commandant of the Regimental Centre who also gave Lothé his heartfelt congratulations. As the Gurkha was the only man to have made such a dramatic escape, those others captured in 1942 still either prisoners of war or stranded in the jungle with Chinese guerillas, his evidence in the case of Mohan Singh gained a special significance.

June 1945, Red Fort, Delhi

But, sadly, all was to turn to dust. So much political pressure was put on the viceroy, Lord Wavell, and the commander-in-chief, Field Marshal Auchinleck, by Pandit Nehru and other Congress leaders, not to press too severe charges against the ring leaders of the INA movement, let alone any lesser mortals, that even the slightest doubt about anyone's evidence against the ring leaders meant that it was not to be allowed to be used against them.

Unaware of any of that, Lothé waited in one of the temporary huts that had sprung up around New Delhi, ready to give his evidence so justice could be done for what he had suffered.

But it was not to be. He was told that he had been categorised 'grey' so his evidence could not be accepted.

Next morning the body of a Gurkha was found hanging in the washroom. It was recognised as Lothé's. It was taken down and the pockets of the clothes searched.

Inside one was a handwritten note, written in pencil with letters not well formed. It was short and to the point: 'The British taught me to keep faith. The British did not keep faith themselves. I have no wish to live any longer as I am not regarded as a man who can be trusted.'

Had he stayed alive assuredly the gangrene from the night soil bucket would have been little to that which he had experienced at the hands of the people he had trusted implicitly for so long: mental and moral turpitude had, sadly, beaten him literally to death.

Deserved but not Dashed

Naik Nakam Gurung, also of 2/1 GR, was ill from malaria when his company commander, Captain Wylie, had to look for a position to his front. He said he would return but never did. Nakam's platoon commander likewise went forward having told Nakam he would return, but he never did either. Soon Nakam was alone. He had been left some rations.

Days turned into weeks, then into months. Only the man himself and the angel that looks after wild animals and soldiers on operations knew how he managed. About six months later he had given up hope. He had probably heard disquieting rumours during one of his desultory contacts for essentials from some frightened villagers and formed his own conclusions.

One day, sitting in a cleft in the branches of a big tree where he had made himself a shelter, waiting for whoever would come to fetch him, he was in such a mood of black despair that he decided to end his life.

His first attempt was to shoot himself but his rifle misfired. His second attempt was to plait a vine rope to hang himself with. But it broke when he jumped off and he hurt his leg as he fell heavily from the height. 'I am ordained to live,' he thought.

He was visited periodically by Chinese guerillas and slowly the years passed. In 1945 the war came to an end but the Chinese guerillas, by now against the British, did not tell Nakam. In 1948 the Malayan Emergency began and he just kept on farming the patch of jungle he had cleared. The aircraft he heard flying overhead were still operating against the Japanese he was told. During those years he never had any salt to eat.

One day in 1949 a patrol of 1/10 GR came into his patch and presumed he was an unarmed guerilla. As Nakam did not run away there was no need for the patrol to open fire. The soldiers approached him and, talking among themselves, noted what a scruffy-looking *daku* – *dacoit*, the Gurkhas' word for guerilla – the man was.

The lone man suddenly realised with a surge of hope flooding all other emotions that the men around him were speaking his language so had come to fetch him. This the patrol commander did not believe when Nakam told him, merely saying that he was a spy and should be shot. But first he asked Nakam who had told him to wait.

And now a curious and unbelievable coincidence occurred: the adjutant of the patrol's battalion was the same Wylie who, in a different battalion, in a different army, was now fighting a different war. 'Wylie sahib,' came the answer.

'That's our adjutant sahib,' and, slightly grudgingly, they took Nakam back with them, again threatening to shoot him if he was lying.

So, after such a long time and in such unexpected circumstances, Wylie and Nakam met. 'I knew you would not forget to send for me,' said Nakam as the two men embraced, both in tears. Nor was Nakam ever to know that the patrol was, in fact, 10 degrees off its correct bearing when it met him.

The tailpiece occurred in 1953 when Wylie, returning from the conquest of Everest, which he helped with Sherpas and oxygen, visited his old battalion, then in Agra. He met Nakam at the camp entrance, now the police havildar.

Still serving? Nakam was asked. Yes, he was because although he had got his back pay, time in the jungle had not counted for pension – so why waste all those years waiting in the jungle?

(Nakam's far too short piece about this, in the regimental history, differs slightly from what I have written above, which Charles Wylie told me himself.)

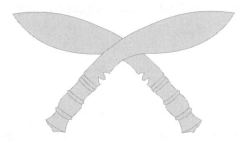

Friend or Fiend?

Animals die with dignity when left alone: mankind, however, is burdened with a need for correct obsequies to be observed, otherwise the soul has no resting place, so we are taught in most, if not all, religions – one definition of which is, after all, 'behaviour focused on salvation'. Many people scoff at the idea of spiritual leftovers after a body becomes a corpse, namely ghosts, but, once the idea of a benevolent deity, or spirit, is accepted, it is logical to accept the opposite idea of a spirit with indifference if not malevolence. It seems that the nearer one is born to the extreme ends of the social pole – throne or soil – the more care is taken in correct disposal of remains. The vast, amorphous mass of us in the middle do not seem to worry nearly so much. I do not write that just to be macabre or melancholy but, observing the rituals for the dead in Nepal, I am now more than ever convinced there is, quite literally, more than meets the eye. I have come across fewer examples of friendly benevolence than fiendish malevolence (certainly, in my own case, my own dearly loved elder brother, killed in the Second World War, has helped me significantly during critical times by advising me what to do in my dreams). The first story is of the former (and all those involved are well known to me); the other four short examples are of what can happen when the dead are not properly prepared for that last journey of all.

There was nothing extraordinary about young Mandhoj Gurung when he was a lad in the village. By the age of 9 he was already good mannered and hard working, like so many other boys. He lived with his parents in a village at the foot of a large mountain in Lamjung and below his house was a strip of thick, almost precipitous, forest that contained caves where wild animals would have their lair.

One day the lad went out to work in the fields but did not return that night, nor the next day. He was not at the houses of the neighbours, nor was it the recruiting season when he might have been tempted to run away without telling his folk.

The local shaman was called in to see if he could help. When the moment was right this man went into a trance and, shaking, invoked the deities and spirits of the surrounding forest to let him know if they knew where young Mandhoj had disappeared. A reassuring answer was given: the lad is safe and unharmed, with a spirit of the forests, a *ban jhañkri*, and he will come back in due course. With that the parents had to be satisfied.

Next morning, Mandhoj did come back, happy, smiling and well fed. He had left the house as normal but, instead of coming back, had woken up in a cave somewhere in the forest, warm, comfortable and extremely happy. He had been well looked after, quite by who or what he was unable to say, and had been fed with delicious food, but again quite what it was he could not describe. But he had been taught how to read divinations, how to see into the future, how to communicate with the … and here he faltered as it seems he was not sure whether they were spirits of the dead or of the unborn.

In fact, he did manage to use his skills so effectively that he was soon acclaimed as the best in the area. He prophesied that one illiterate lad would become a captain in the British Army, and indeed this man, against the odds of late promotion at every rank, finished as a Gurkha major, honorary captain and senior area recruiting officer, and was made MBE.

For another he said that, if this man were to go overseas he would have nothing but trouble. In the event this man got as far as Singapore in the Gurkha contingent but so poor was his health that he was soon discharged. The day he boarded the ship back to Calcutta he started to recover his health and, by the time he was back in the hills, he was completely cured. His illness was never diagnosed. Back in the village he asked Mandhoj what would happen if he joined the Indian Army, and was told that he would have two great crises during his service, one in the army and one at home, but would get no pension.

So, with trepidation for the future overlaid with the challenges of the moment, he joined the 5th Gorkhas. In the early 1960s he was nearly killed in action and shortly afterwards captured a Pakistani spy, a major masquerading as an apple seller, then had to go home to help bury an elder brother. Just before he was due out on pension as a subedar he was promoted to honorary captain, which he still is, but, for some reason best known to others, was only allowed an honorary lieutenant's pension – so it was he left the army 'with no pension' (but only of his latest rank!).

His daughter was an unlucky girl in that she was born on the night of the new moon. Unless the husband's divinations were exactly right, there would be a tragedy. So Mandhoj (himself on pension from the Assam Rifles) was approached and asked what was best to do. There were two options: take the first 'correct' man from the east and risk tragedy of another family member soon afterwards; or ignore the omens and have a tragedy with his daughter. For the former it so happened that the younger of my two 'godsons' qualified, coming from the east and having correct divinations – it was also a love marriage. Three weeks after the wedding the girl's grandfather died prematurely.

Mandhoj is stone deaf but still works in the fields and is still highly respected.

At the very end of 1962, while operating in the north-east of Malaya, in Temiar aborigine territory, one of my soldiers, Rifleman Netrabahadur Rai, was drowned in a deep, fast-flowing river, the Blaur, downstream from where I was. We were in one of the remotest areas of Malaya, three weeks' walk from the road head. Although the emergency was over, we were still on operations against the rump of the communist terrorists. That was the second death by drowning in as many weeks. What was left of his body was recovered some days later and was buried nearby.

By then I had been in the jungle for nearly a year, not quite non-stop, and was run down. I was ordered down to the platoon of the dead soldier to conduct another inquiry. My camp had been chosen by one who had not realised it was in the middle of an aborigine graveyard. I could not spare any escort from my own group of nine Gurkhas so took one Temiar with me as escort. Three days later I was back.

I greeted the men left behind and learnt all was well. I told them I was going down to the river we got our water from – not the main one, the Blaur – to wash, as I was hot, uncomfortable and very tired. The washing place was 20 yards or so above a waterfall, which fell many feet into a deep pool. I stood on a small upraised stone soaping myself and suddenly heard maniacal laughter. I looked up and saw no one. I heard it again and, as I looked up, I completely lost my balance as though I had been pushed in the chest. I was swept down towards the waterfall and arrested myself only feet from its edge. I waded back, determined not to pay attention to such things, and started soaping myself again, standing on the stone: more maniacal laughter, another push, once again gasping and being swept to the very lip of the waterfall. I just managed to clamber out and I went back to my stone, this time keeping my feet out of the water on the side. I had no false pride and I was sure one of my men had been playing a joke on me. I finished washing and returned to the camp and angrily demanded an explanation. 'Who was laughing at me and why?'

I was met by the most genuine of blank surprises. 'Not us,' they chorused. Nor was it Temiar, nor Chinese guerillas. It was later explained to me by one of the Temiar elders: by living on their old burial ground, what else could we expect? But was it either of the two dead Gurkhas or a Temiar? It had been the practice for many years for a Temiar community to move when someone died of illness. This entailed burning down the flimsy wooden houses and, it was hoped, the disease. Once I was asked if my soldiers could help burn down one of the houses, which we did. Twenty yards away we heard the fleas jumping – click, click – as they tried to escape. Placating the homeless spirit, which would wander through the jungle, sometimes hooting like an owl, deciding where or whether to build temporary or more permanent huts, when to start felling the jungle and many other details were all the shaman's responsibilities. In this case the local community had been forbidden to move away from where they were after a death, so the spirits were unsettled. By then I had been many months in the jungle and was probably as tired mentally as I was physically: could it have been lack of normal mental resilience that made me a target?

Whoever it was, or had been, that explanation solved other curious happenings: my hammock, tied between two stout trees, being pushed from side to side violently with no man present and no wind, and when I was inside; men knocked off the bamboo platforms they had made to sit on, with no other man in reach; and candles being blown out, also with no wind. How else would these have happened? It was most eerie. Was it only the dead Temiar not liking us? The atmosphere was redolent with unease by then and we all felt it. And yet, when I slept in a graveyard in Nepal, where the obsequies had been correctly performed, I was not haunted.

On operations in the jungle I had a golden rule that, when there was a halt, no one would move for five minutes. This was in case a guerilla was in the immediate vicinity and would otherwise be aware of our presence by cigarette smoke if not by noise. One day it paid off. A guerilla – an armed and uniformed Chinese youth – walked straight into us and was shot. He fell to the ground. I went over to him to give succour and he died as I was touching him; the death rattle, convulsing his throat, spent itself in the silence of the jungle.

I searched his belongings and found a new shirt and trousers, fifty-two new exercise books, a saw, nine maps, five letters and many diaries. While a grave was being dug for him I stripped him, searching for any telltale tattoos or birthmarks, the better to recognise him. I also photographed him and took his fingerprints. I told headquarters of what had happened.

That evening I was astonished to get a message telling me to take the body back to the nearest rubber estate (six hours' walk away) whence the guerilla had come. In vain did I remonstrate, saying that he was obviously a courier moving the same way as we were, towards the central gang, which we were looking for. To alert the rubber estate's population that their contact had been killed could easily nullify much of the information waiting to be culled from the papers I had found. The soldiers, too, were unhappy with this task, for although the body had only been buried a few hours, it would be an unpleasant and exhausting task: it had to be exhumed and carried back through the jungle, with a path being hacked out.

Higher formation was adamant, so I detached a platoon and sent them back with the corpse. When they eventually arrived at the estate boundary it was as I had gloomily prophesied: the news spread like wildfire and everybody knew that troops were operating in the area (a secret up till then). The brigadier later had the grace to admit that he made a wrong decision.

During the next few days I found my strength and appetite waning. By the time we were out of the jungle I was quite weak. I went back to base, 30 miles of winding hills away, by scout car. That type of vehicle held three people: a driver and two Bren gunners. The arrangement for the gunners was simple: twin-mounted light machine guns were fixed on to a metal stalk outside the scout car on the roof and operated by remote control handlebars from inside. The seat this gunner sat on could be elevated, so when the sliding lid-like roof was open, the whole was raised sufficiently for his head to protrude. This was cooler than being cooped up inside. The second gunner sat right down in the front of the scout car, next to the driver, at the feet of the first gunner.

Soon after we started I began to feel uncomfortable. By the time we were winding over the top of a mountain pass I felt I had to vomit. I stopped the driver, jumped out and retched emptily. I sat gloomily by the side of the road while the two Gurkhas waited patiently. Presently they suggested we move on. Once again, in the scout car I felt we were moving with incredible speed. 'Slow down, slow down!' I begged the driver. Apparently we were moving very slowly. I felt fish-belly cold and lowered my seat to get warm. A dizziness assailed me and I must have started behaving queerly. The driver turned to the second driver and said something I could not fully catch, ' … had affected him.' An impulse made me bend forward and embrace the gunner for warmth and everything became topsy-turvy. I dimly heard his answer, 'But he is a Christian. His *girja* [Church] will protect him.'

'The effect has worn off: he has been with us a long time.'

'Will you try?'

'Yes, but it may not work.'

I did not understand what the two men were discussing – try what? I was told to sit up and, shakily, I did. The driver, Kalibahadur Limbu, leant back and snicked some earth from my shoes on to his finger, then scratched some polish off both toecaps. Because I had work to do in Seremban I had dressed nicely but my shoes had got muddy when I left the vehicle earlier.

Kalibahadur spat on the mixture and made a paste of it. He started muttering and I was too uninterested and remote to care how he was driving or to listen to what he was saying. He dabbed my forearms with the paste, my forehead and the tip of my tongue. 'That should do it,' he told his companion.

Almost immediately I felt a ball inside the pit of my stomach pushing up and up. I gasped as it struggled against my throat, choking me. As it burst through I started sobbing out loud. It took me completely by surprise and lasted only a few seconds. I pulled myself together and, feeling warmer, told the driver to drive normally.

Kalibahadur, a shaman in his own right, increased his speed, saying nothing. Within ten minutes I felt very much better, although utterly worn out. I was to learn that the guerilla's soul had entered into mine when I touched him as he died. Apparently, I was only partially affected because the Christian influence of the Church had not completely been negated by my association with Hindu and Buddhist Gurkhas.

I never did learn how the soul of the dead guerilla was finally put to rest. However, any Christian priest who has exorcised another's spirit from the body other than its own will describe the same symptoms that I experienced.

Two companies of 1/7 GR were on detachment, some 50 miles from battalion HQ, sharing a camp with a Jungle Company of the Royal Malay Police. All was tranquil until, some months later, the occupants of one hut were, one by one, woken up as a hand came in under their mosquito net and pinched the end of their member. Suspicions were rife and one man was suspected. A guard was put on his bed the next night and the man slept the whole night through without waking – yet in another barrack room the same thing happened. Each man was similarly awoken by a pinching of his member and a suspect presumed – the same man.

There was murmuring among the soldiers and an undercurrent of great disquiet filtered everywhere as news of this unprecedented occurrence was discussed in quiet whispers. Smiles had left faces. No one knew what would happen but happen it would. How could a man, asleep in bed all night and guarded by men who were ready to take the severest action, have got out to carry on with this unnatural and unheard-of task? It could not therefore be the man himself; it had to be his soul, his *hangsa*.

It was not long before Dashera and all had, by then, come out of the jungle. Two days before Mar (the day the bull is beheaded during the Dashera ceremony) the senior Gurkha officer came to me and told me he had ordered all kukris to be gathered inside the *kot*. Trouble was in the air: we were located where we were in order to kill guerillas, not one another.

A convoy of four lorries left our camp very early on the morning of Mar, to celebrate it in battalion HQ. I, in my own car, left before the convoy did. It was very late in arriving; there had been an accident: a lorry had, most unexpectedly, overturned and one man had been killed when a canopy strut had crushed him, the company second-in-command told me. I asked who had died and learnt it was he who had been suspected of the pinching.

Just then I was called to the telephone and an angry police lieutenant gave me a torrent of abuse as he described what one of my soldiers had done the night before. He had got into the Malay Police family quarters and, snuggling between man and wife as they lay there, made himself at home. He demanded the man be punished and an official apology.

I apologised and told him that the man who had done it was dead. But had that man been responsible?

Brigade HQ was situated in a place where many wounded Australian soldiers and Chinese civilians had been massacred by the Japanese.

The communications centre was sited at one edge of the camp, next to the road and opposite a piece of land on which rank grass grew.

One morning a soldier, wanting to have a breath of fresh air and to stretch his legs, wandered on to the grass and urinated. A searing pain, like an electric current, ran up the jet into the man's body. He remembered no more.

His legs took him back into the communication centre, where his distraught condition and his inability to talk made the person in charge put him in a vehicle and have him sent back to his own lines, with an escort who was to tell the Gurkha major about it.

As soon as the man was taken to his barrack room he fell asleep, only to awake in the evening. To everybody's utter amazement, he understood none, nor could he speak any, of his mother tongue – only Chinese. Consternation was rife as it was known that the man was not a Chinese speaker.

The Gurkha major sent a representative down to the scene of the original occurrence and, asking around the local population, discovered that the man must have urinated on an unmarked Chinese grave. The problem had to be solved.

A Chinese shaman was located in the town. He agreed to go and carry out long-delayed obsequies on the Chinese grave. He then went to the camp and, in the presence of a Gurkha shaman, spoke to the disturbed soldier, who understood him and not the other.

The Chinese shaman blew over him, muttered mantras around him and lit candles for him. The soldier stayed silent. It was then the turn of the Gurkha shaman to do likewise. A watch was put on the soldier for the rest of the night but there was nothing for him to do as the soldier slept soundly.

When he awoke in the morning, he was as fluent as ever in Gurkhali and could not understand it when a Chinese speaker was brought in to talk to him because, as he pointed out, he had never learnt that language. All he remembered was a searing pain but was too embarrassed to say where or how it had happened.

Even if you were only to say 'pon my soul', there could be something in it all, even for the most sceptical!

Monsoon 1988

The monsoon in Nepal is regarded both as an unspoken benison of the gods and a curse. Monsoon 1988 saw both aspects. Without the rains nature will dry up and life become unsupportable; when there is too much and it is too violent, generations of labour will be washed away as hillsides crumble and crash into the valleys. Death and destruction are an ever-present threat. People do not expect to travel in the monsoon and the last time that friends from other villages can safely meet is at the festival of *Chaité Dasaiñ* that takes place, with fairs and fun, some time in April. In the six-seasoned Nepalese calendar the rainy season is only from mid June to mid August, although wet conditions pertain for much longer. During this period there will be days of drizzle, of heavy rain, of mud, of leeches, of cloud and of blazing sunshine, hotter than before the rains started now that the haze and dust of the drier months have been washed away.

This year, as normal, after the first rains had softened the soil sufficiently, ploughing took place. People have just discovered that there is such a thing as a curved blade that puts the soil on to one side and which makes a better, quicker and easier plough for both man and beast. Some farmers have started to use only one bullock – a revolution, indeed, in its own fashion. Others say that the strain is too much for one animal, so still use two. Rice seedlings are planted in nurseries. It is a matter of nice judgement when to start transplanting them: fields have to be flooded and the soil made into the correct muddy consistency before groups of villagers take to the fields, helping each other out on a rota basis. The menfolk are responsible for coaxing the oxen to flatten the soil with wooden rollers. The planting is the job of the womenfolk and mighty tired they must feel at the end of a long day, with back aching, feet and legs caked in mud and hands aching. The prettiness of the scene is only in the eye of the beholder.

The first day of the monsoon is the equivalent of St Swithin's Day in Britain except that in Nepal it needs to rain in both morning and evening for the monsoon to be a good one. In 1988, certainly in Pokhara, this occurred. The almanac that predicts fair weather and foul did have a warning for calamities. Its prognostications were, as always, duly Delphic, but it did predict a major earthquake and was only one day out.

The Pokhara valley has the largest rainfall in the kingdom, along with Lumlé, taking the brunt of the water. Unlike many other places, the pre-monsoon heat is often alleviated by fierce storms that lash the landscape; almost horizontal winds hit houses and often rip roofs that have not been weighted down by large stones. 'The mountains make their own weather,' it is said and, with the Himalayas seemingly almost near enough to put the hand out to touch, those living in the valley are at their mercy.

At the start of this rainy season there was a remarkable event in Ram Bazaar, the village to the south of Pokhara town. Rajendra Gurung, the son of an ex-Gurkha Transport Regiment (GTR) soldier, was fêted by the villagers as being the best student in the countrywide School Leaving Certificate exam. We were told about it two evenings before. We assembled at the chosen site in the middle of the village and all the local dignitaries, both of the administration and from Rajendra's school, the Gandaki Boarding School, were present, as well as a goodly sprinkling of villagers. Apparently it was the first time that this honour had gone outside the valley – certainly if the British Army school in Hong Kong is not taken into consideration – and everybody was justly proud of it. Speeches were made lauding this attainment, money was raised for the continuation of the lad's education, garlands were placed round his neck and a gracious reply was given in appreciation. As a spontaneous show of pride and goodwill it was most unusual and memorable. Only the day was damp, cloudy and dull.

By the middle of the monsoon the rice sowing had all but been completed. The sickly yellow wisps would soon be that loveliest of colours, the deep emerald green of growing rice. I always find the extra dimension of seeing the sky and the mountains reflected in the paddy fields (no relation to the Irishman of the same name!) particularly attractive. Around where I live with my Nepalese family there runs a deep and swift river (Seti Khola) that flows from Machha Puchharé Himal. Only in the dry season, though glacier-cold, is the river fordable. After rain it is impossible to cross and so are many of the smaller rivers that join it. Most days my surrogate son and I go for a walk, seldom shorter than three hours and often longer. One morning in late May we thought we could still cross one of the smaller rivers without going round by a long detour. Locals shook their heads and watched us with clinical detachment as it swept us off our feet and we had to swim for it. The three dogs we take with us (two ours and one a neighbour's) were swept much farther downstream than were we. However, we all emerged, wet to the skin, having learnt our lesson!

Much of the countryside to the south of Pokhara is like a split-level maze. There are deep gorges and precipitous cliffs of around 100ft that make walking not only hazardous but also difficult. It takes time to learn about the tiny paths up and down them that, at first sight, do not exist. As the ground softens, chunks of rock and shale crash or slither away, to the eternal discomfort of any man or beast who happens to be there at the time.

There is a variety of wildlife: monkeys, jackals, civet cats and mongooses, to say nothing of vultures. One evening, when the rain had left off, I took the dogs for a walk and saw an animal that I did not recognise. I asked some locals and some said it was a hare, yet others said it was a jackal. I have, to my intense interest, discovered that it is neither. It is a Burmese ferret badger (there is also a Chinese variety that is lighter in colour), which lives in burrows on flat ground, is nocturnal and feeds on grubs. The dogs go mad when they find one. The dogs also love chasing the monkeys who, at this time of year, are great predators, not having had much food during the period before the monsoon. Maize is what the monkeys seem to like. They stalk up to the fields, sending out sentries to see if there are any enemies before the main flock comes up behind them. Around most of the fields small boys and girls sit disconsolately in the rain with, if they are lucky, a home-made umbrella made of plaited grasses. At the rear of any flock of monkeys come the mothers and babies. Recently one of my dogs chased some monkeys near the lip of a precipice, which is their favourite hiding place as nothing can touch them there. Under the lip were some babies trying, not very successfully, to find their way up towards their mother who, with true maternal devotion, mouthed her dislike of the dog and jumped on to him, sending him away at speed, tail between his legs. Alas, I had no camera with me.

As I said, people normally do not want to travel far in the monsoon but, for me at least, 1988 was an exception. Towards the end of August I went for a walk in the eastern hills to meet old friends and chat about the reasons behind the plan to move out from the camp for recruiting-cum-pension paying in Dharan. I had moved the western equivalent from Paklihawa to Pokhara in 1979 and the worries and anxieties of those affected by such a traumatic event were very real to them. In that case we in the west could fall back on Dharan for certain facilities, such as the hospital and resettlement courses. Capping the wellsprings of discontent was hard enough then: now it would be harder still to calm fears of abandonment at worst, disenchantment at best. A new-look solution, despite retention of the hospital under different management for a limited period, is under active consideration. There has, obviously, been a lot of planning and, equally clearly, there has yet to be a lot more, yet until these plans have been finalised and made public, only outline detains could be given. One of the misapprehensions our ex-servicemen are under is that the move is connected to the move out of Hong Kong in 1997. The smoothness of that operation was very much dependent on the maintenance of Gurkha morale. But, with or without the Hong Kong factor, the place Dharan has outlived its original rationale, namely to be at the end of the Indian railhead in a country without any roads or air facilities. Thirty years ago the Terai was the area to aim for: now Kathmandu and the use of the new road network (still to be developed in the east) makes a large camp in the east redundant.

I had last wandered the eastern hills twelve years before and found the whole area much more relaxed than I had known it, on and off, since 1967. News of the closure of Ghopa camp in Dharan had reverberated around the eastern hills, causing many people, ex-servicemen and civilians, to wonder what it was all about and whether the British were abandoning them, thus ending many years of British connection.

The weather was the worst I had ever come across in my 10,000 miles in all-weather walking in Nepal. One night, when we had changed out of our wet clothes and were regaling ourselves with some scaldingly hot tea, the conversation turned to how one should always remember one's station in life (this in connection with modern Nepalese society and some members thereof trying to better themselves) and I was treated to a new fable:

A mouse wanted to better his family so he asked if his daughter could marry the sun, the biggest object he could think of. 'I'm not that big,' said the sun, 'a cloud will obscure me. Ask the cloud for his hand in marriage.'

The cloud declined and blamed the wind for not being able always to stay big enough to obscure the sun. 'Try the wind,' was the advice given to the mouse.

The wind declined saying that the hills checked his course and suggested that a big hill was approached. But the answer there was that the mouse, singly or in his thousands, could weaken the fabric of the hills by burrowing, so causing devastating landslides, and that the only answer was for mouse to marry mouse. So this is what, sadly and maybe wisely, happened.

We were in cloud, mist or rain for twenty-six out of thirty-four days. It was on the morning of the tenth day of our walk that the earthquake struck.

We were in a house by the Dudh Kosi and were all awoken by a loud, grating, stuttering noise. Our beds shook and we bolted outside. Luckily nothing in that vicinity fell down although there were cracks in the older houses. The wide river was momentarily hurled off course. In fact, we saw no major damage until we were halfway between Diktel and Khotang, the Sampsu Khola being the dividing line. The only good effect of the earthquake, apart from international goodwill shown, was that I met far more folk than I would otherwise have done as they came in to report damage to property and livestock. I therefore had a much wider audience than expected and could spread my reassuring message that, despite their fears and rumours to the contrary, the British were not abandoning the East.

The glamour and vainglory of regimental soldiering over the years of four decades had long faded but the magic of camaraderie then formed, dormant for so long, instantly and without hesitation rose to the surface everywhere I went. At eight welfare centres, in villages or on the way, names and numbers, in the main, sprang to the mind and almost everybody had his own anecdote about the times we had spent together – some true and flattering, some untrue and flattering, others neither! Looking at the men's animated faces and shining eyes was like looking into a mirror: the once smooth-faced, clean-limbed and upright lads were sometimes scarcely recognised now that they had become shriven, wrinkled, toothless and grey-haired or bald. I, too, after so much time, was one of that large army of 'those who fade away'.

In all I suppose I spoke to between 450 and 500 people about the future, including 141 in Dharan, and I got the firm impression that everybody with whom I spoke accepted what I told them wholeheartedly. As I spoke to around 10 per cent of eastern hill and Dharan-based pensioners, I regard this acceptance as of great significance.

But that aside it was the reactions of one ill man and one old woman I had gone to meet that held the attention of the soldier who was with us and my Nepalese godson. The man lived in Bagsila (whither I had made a detour to visit the widow of an old friend whose two sons I had helped over the years). I was told he was ill and, from behind his house, I called his regimental number, rank and name. I found him sitting forlornly on a wooden bed in the front of his house, clutching a stool to keep himself upright. His face was puffy, he coughed and wheezed and was obviously very unhappy and very ill.

He did not grumble at his fate nor did he bewail the effects on his family but told me his troubles as though he were reporting how he had been on patrol in yesteryear. I reminded him of our time together in the early 1950s on operations in the jungle in Malaya. That started him off. For over an hour he was back in time, reliving old actions, quoting old remarks, even singing an old song as the years rolled back and his illness was forgotten. He clutched a sickle in his hands, twisting the handle vigorously as bandit after bandit was met and dispatched. He needed no prompting. His family stared at him in wonder and delight.

'Never did I think we would meet again. I can now die happy,' he said as I left and he slumped over the stool as loneliness and heartache overtook him once again.

The old woman was the mother of a friend I had served with in the Gurkha Independent Parachute Company and with whom I had walked the eastern hills twenty-three years before. I had stayed with her in Bhojpur, she a widow even then, and had met her again seven years later when she had started to go blind. Her son, pensioned, had gone to Kathmandu several times to try to find me, so I was told, but had failed. With the son having suddenly died of a heart attack eighteen months before, his mother was still bereft.

She was sleeping when I went to see her. I woke her up. 'Mother, the friend of your son has come to meet you,' I called. She bade me sit down beside her and then she poured her heart out, weeping copiously as she did. I held her hand and muttered soothing words but could not stop the flow. I then had an idea to take her mind off her sadness. 'Mother, was it in 1959 or 1958 that you made that journey to Kathmandu by yourself?'

'Neither: it was in 1957 and I took my youngest with me ...'

For ninety minutes the old lady gave me chapter and verse as she retraced all her footsteps, giving graphic accounts of the hardships of the journey – how she once went for five days with only water to drink, how she was ignored, misled, how folk tried to rob her – but she had prevailed and been successful, even if her people hardly recognised her when she got back home, months later, because she was so thin and weary. For sheer pluck and guts I have seldom heard such a story, and I wished I could have made a recording of it. She did not need any prompting: she sat bolt upright, eyes dry, a clarity in her diction and a hardness in her voice that belied her frail body. She went on and on and on.

It was time to go. Gently I told her it was getting dark and I had to leave. At that she came back from the past into the present, she slumped and started to weep. Can I accept her invitation to come again and stay?

By the first week in September the rains had slackened and we had three days of sunshine, even seeing the Himalayas for the first time – just for five minutes. On 12–13 September it rained all night and at least two complete hillsides collapsed, softened by endless rain and jolted by the earthquake and the tremors that came for fourteen days afterwards. Overnight, rivers were filled with soil, turning their approaches into mud that, thigh–deep, was glutinous enough to entrap a single traveller. The grit and stones in the black, evil–looking water made the river roar when normally there would have been a happy ripple. The intensity of the flow and the thickness of the dirt took little chunks out of the skin of our legs. Many were the detours we had to make where the path had been swept into the valley below the night before and many more were the places that, sooner than later, would also crumble. It was frightening to behold. Nature can be unpredictably cruel.

On our way from Kathmandu to Jiri by vehicle, the road had been torn away from its moorings both by river water eroding the foundations and the land above it collapsing. It would have to wait until the cold weather before it could be repaired properly. As we walked along the Dhankuta–Dharan road we again saw evidence of the fury of the water and the power it has to make a mockery of what man has done over many months and years by undoing it in a matter of minutes.

Yes, it was a different monsoon.

Two Vows

1:Vice

The barren, boulder-strewn, steep hillside where he had been born was five days' hard walk away when the man who had left home to make good found himself tired and hungry, near his destination, but at the bottom of a steep hill. He travelled light but, even so, found the way up the hill a strain as there was nowhere he could rest till he reached the top and the track was difficult with loose stones. He envisaged a resting place halfway, just where he had noticed a cooling breeze (for it was mid *Chait* (end of April) and the weather had turned hot). 'When I have my first son,' he mused, 'I will pay for a flagged path and a resting place to be made.' He saw in his mind's eye the square stone platform (*chautara*), with the shelf all around it where a man could easily rest his load.

Two trees were always planted together on a *chautara*, the *bar* and the *pipal*. Custom, from time immemorial, has required these trees be married by the priests, just like man and woman, with correctly read divinations found from the almanac. He daydreamed further: 'How wonderful if my son's marriage and that of the trees coincided.' As he lulled himself to sleep that night he mentally completed the picture by envisaging the little stone-flagged tank some yards in front of the *chautara* with the carved wooden pole so essential to ritual, sticking up in the water. Unluckily his eldest son and the trees were far too young to be married when he unexpectedly died.

The years passed. The son grew up under his mother's care but his father's dream of a joint marriage never materialised. There was only enough money for his marriage, none for the two trees. 'Never mind,' he thought. 'My eldest son's birth will be an occasion for this to happen.'

However, despite all hopes, he did not sire a son and heir, only a daughter. He was a diligent worker and by the standards of the time, some sixty years previous, was rich. He told his friends about his hopes and daydreams when he took counsel with them on how to remedy such matters. It was pronounced that he should make a vow for the *bar* and the *pipal* to be properly and expensively married and he would be blessed with a son.

Now there were two servants, nicknamed Gophlé (the one with chubby cheeks) and Sikuté (the thin one), trusted implicitly, but who were, unfortunately, filled with greed at their master's richness. They were cunning, clever and low-minded, contriving to act both at the marriage ceremony and for its preparation in such a way that they could get their hands on the money and escape with it. In this they were successful and both managed to get away unscathed, with enough money to make themselves significantly richer than those with whom they eventually found themselves.

The fury of the deprived man was only matched by the disappointment, at remaining unrewarded, of those whose counsels he had needed. A curse was put on both the thieves that they too should never have any sons and that, however successful their money might seem to make them, they be doomed to disappointment.

More years passed. Sikuté married and built a house. The house was robbed and later collapsed in an earthquake. His fowls were continuously taken by jackals and his one daughter was born mentally impaired. She grew up, married, had a family and all, less the son-in-law, were mortally stricken. The son-in-law remarried and had eight children, five being 'touched by the gods'. The villagers shunned them and shed no tear when three of them, along with their grandfather, died. Somehow or other the curse was known of implicitly, if never discussed explicitly. The house in which the remnants of the family lived was ill-starred and even when Sikuté's son-in-law and second wife died within two days of one another, the unintelligible prattle and dangerous tantrums of the two remaining hapless ones were grim reminders of the folly of the act of greed that prevented a significant act of devotion.

Gophlé moved to a different area and likewise produced no son. A similar catalogue as Sikuté's would be tedious; suffice it to say that he was still alive then and despised and shunned by other villagers as being a loud-mouthed, cantankerous bully who still lived under the strain of the curse.

'How do you know all this?' I asked my companion at the end of this involved story.

'One of the thieves was my grandfather,' he replied, 'and you saw what my uncles were like in my village before we moved to last night's place. It so happened that the other thief was the owner of the house we were staying in last night.'

2:Virtue

In a land constantly menaced by landslides and soil erosion, scraping a living from the soil is precarious. The widow and her only son had moved back to where her husband had come from, soon after his death. Life was hard and the son, Narbahadur Rai, joined the army as soon as he was old enough. He sent his mother as much money as he could and by dint of a good record had reached Gurkha captain when I joined the battalion. He had married late for a Gurkha, after the Burma War, and had a large and contented family. His youngest son, aged 6, was the apple of his father's eye.

After he had retired on pension (he died in 1986) Narbahadur was elected the village leader. Among other things he soon had a school built for primary classes and two teachers were engaged. Many problems of the villagers came his way and, although frequently exasperated, he was a popular and successful arbiter. His fame spread and the village was to be honoured by an unusually high official visiting it.

Great activity ensued. Village paths were repaired, broken walls restored and the school re-decorated. Outside the school was a large boulder that was not embedded in the ground but lay slightly on a tilt. It offended Narbahadur's sense of tidiness, as the gap had become a collecting place for waste. He decided to try to get it flush with the ground so he arranged for a group of twenty-four men armed with crowbars to move it. It was a feat to find enough crowbars for the job but, try hard as they might, they could not budge the boulder at all.

Narbahadur's youngest son was a spectator to this and, on the morrow, when all the men were away doing something else, he crawled into the gap between boulder and ground to remove the rubbish and thereby please his father. No sooner was he underneath when the boulder, obviously loosened by the exertions of the previous day, subsided. An indentation in the ground allowed just enough room for the little boy's head to be undamaged, but not so his body, which was almost, but not quite, crushed outright.

Some little girls playing nearby rushed to get help when they saw what had happened, but with all the men away the womenfolk were unable to organise themselves. Narbahadur's eldest daughter, however, saw the need for immediate action. In desperation, she told all the other little girls to run back to the scene of the accident and try to move the boulder by themselves. Their search for help had taken twenty minutes, an uncomfortably long time under the circumstances, but a muffled bleat from the little boy showed he was still alive, albeit probably hideously broken. So, armed with pieces of wood, a dozen little girls, aged between 8 and 12, tried with might and main to shift the boulder. With superhuman strength, they managed to lift it sufficiently high and just long enough for one little girl to snatch the trapped boy from underneath before the sheer weight of rock exerted its overpowering pressure and it again subsided.

The lad was laid on the ground, purple-faced with near suffocation, as his father rushed to the scene. Narbahadur very gently lifted his son up, even more carefully took his shirt off and, when he realised that the only damage was a large and ugly bruise, unashamedly wept.

'Wasn't that miraculous?' I asked him.

'Yes,' he replied. 'I cannot explain what happened except to say that the gods helped me out. To show my appreciation I have had a *chautara* made and a *bar* and a *pipal* tree planted and have vowed that they be properly married … on the same day as my son, if possible, as my grandfather had once so wished for my father.'

Three Virtues

I: Faith

One winter, in December, a stranger visited the hills of Nepal. A soldier, on leave, had volunteered his services as guide and the two men met each other at the road head. Thence they moved north for six days, spending one night in the soldier's home, to where the hoarfrost lay heavily until the morning sun removed it, high up in the rhododendron and pine forests – serene, fresh and quiet. At the top of the high pass the snows came into view, bleak, timeless and inscrutable. They were soon out of sight as the path led the two men down into the next valley.

The stranger's companion wanted to worship, so the two men decided to visit a famous Buddhist monastery miles to the north. It meant leaving the beaten track and venturing into more remote areas. Their route led through harvested rice fields, now brown, bare and dusty in the winter sunshine, then near a river where an otter was seen fishing. Up and up, until the houses were left behind and the forests reached once more. Through them they walked and then they were on cleared land where only potatoes grew with the air, by now, thin and cold. A shack with a Buddhist pennant outside was reached and a resting place for the night was sought. A night's shelter was given in an outhouse that had walls and roof of plaited wattle.

It was a relief to be moving and to get warm again. Although the pass they had to cross was not really high, they found their breath short and their limbs heavy. Great banks of frozen mist whirled and spun, like smoke from a giant cauldron, leaving fresh streaks of white where they had brushed the hillsides. Near the top of the pass cloud was being driven in three different directions as the cold air from the snows met the warmer air from below. The last two hours lay up the side of a stream, whose banks were thick rimed and where the water was a trickle with solid ice either side. Snow had fallen a while back and, as the place up which they travelled saw little sun, it lay, caked and frozen. Progress was slow, but there was no hurry. The soldier had picked some fern smelling of parsley and said to be efficacious in warding off the spirits found high up. The correct place to put it was behind the ear, but the stranger put it sheepishly in his pocket.

From the pass they saw a settlement in the valley far below them. There were three double-storeyed houses, a number of low shacks, few cattle but many potato fields. Around the settlement was, on one side, a sheer precipice and on the other two sides gentle slopes covered with trees. The fourth side was open, sloping down to a river beyond which rose the snows, much nearer by now. Mount Everest, shielded, lay out of sight.

Outside one of the large houses sat an old woman sorting potatoes. Nearby was a cow, one leg broken shorter than the rest. Shelter for the night was requested and a wattle-girt shed was pointed out. The stranger had noticed that the house had two rooms on the ground floor, one the family room and the other, strewn with leaves, empty save for a ladder up to the top floor. He was invited to inspect the upstairs room. It ran the length of the house and, at the far end, there were three resplendent Buddhas, gilt and large, and a fourth, smaller, red one. They had been brought from China, long years before. Many smaller statues abounded. Grain was also stored along the walls and, in one corner, was an empty bed. Twenty people could have fitted in the room but the stranger was told that in winter the room so caught the wind he could not sleep there.

'May we please sleep in the room with the leaves?' he asked. 'No,' he was told. 'That is reserved for the injured cow. You may have the place outside.'

The night was very cold and very long. Early the next morning the soldier disappeared for a while, carrying towel and soap. He returned, shivering, having totally immersed himself in the freezing water, and he carried a bowl of clarified butter.

'As soon as the lama outside has had his head shaved, I'm going up to the main prayer house to pray,' and he pointed out the largest of the three houses. 'Come along with me, do!'

They went up the hill and reached the building. They waited for three red-robed lamas to come and the door was unlocked. As it was opened the sun streamed in and the stranger was amazed to see a riot of colour. Straight in front of the door, on the opposite wall, was the altar. This consisted of a large gilt Buddha, in front of which were many small ones. There were shallow cups set around a centre stand in which butter was poured, while bowls and jars of many sorts lay in front. Flanking the altar was the library, fifty-four cubby holes either side, each with sacred cloth-covered scriptures peering out in yellow, red and blue symmetry. A pew ran down the centre of the room with conch, cymbals and gong to hand. The walls and ceiling garishly depicted the rise and fall of man. The fallen were shown as having their limbs torn off and being eaten by ravenous demons, as being trampled on and squashed, as being burnt. The risen were sitting in the lotus position, eyes inscrutably contemplating eternity. It was very cold.

By now the three lamas were sitting cross-legged on the bench of the pew. The soldier was standing in front of the altar, head bent, eyes closed, and the stranger was seated by the wall. None wore shoes. A low, murmuring chant started and an acolyte came in and laid fern-like leaves in the vessels in front of the Buddha. The soldier poured

Parachuting: Gurkha Independent Parachute Company Dropping from a RAF Hercules Aircraft near Kluang, Peninsular Malaysia, late 1965

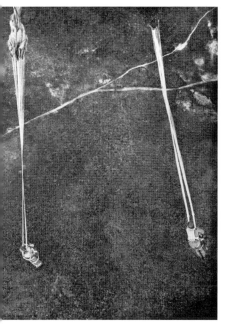

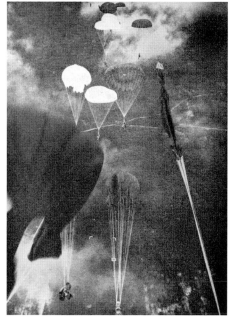

'What's happened to my parachute?' (PR HQ Far East Land Forces)

Happiness is an open parachute … (PR HQ Far East Land Forces)

Major General A.G. Patterson, Brigade of Gurkhas, presenting the red berets of the Parachute Regiment, instead of the normal rifle green berets, to members of the Gurkha Independent Parachute Company, of which the author was OC, on 5 July 1966. (PR HQ Far East Land Forces)

The Honourable East India Company Fought a Famous Battle Against the Gorkhas near Dehra Dun, November 1814

THIS IS INSCRIBED
AS A TRIBUTE OF RESPECT
FOR OUR GALLANT ADVERSARY
BULBUDDER
COMMANDER OF THE FORT
AND HIS BRAVE GOORKAS
WHO WERE AFTERWARDS
WHILE IN THE SERVICE
OF RUNJEET SING
SHOT DOWN IN THEIR RANKS
TO THE LAST MAN
BY AFGHAN ARTILLERY.

The wording to the famous Gorkha, Bulbudder. On the other panel is the name of Major General Robert Gillespie. Seldom, if ever, do brave men of both sides appear on the same monument. (Mrs Madhu Gurung)

Some way off from the original is another, new, monument, commemorating the struggle of 1814. The chairman of the committee who made the monument for the 200th anniversary of Gurkha service is presenting us with a memento. On the left is Lieutenant General Shakti Gurung, the first Gurung to be commissioned to such a high rank in the Indian Army. (Mrs Madhu Gurung)

The Nepalese troops in the fort surrendered to the Hon East Company's army on 18 April 1815 and, from 24 April 1815, 1st, 2nd and 3rd Gurkha Rifles had their origin. The author's surrogate son, Buddhiman Gurung, is a direct descendant of arguably the bravest Gurkha ever, who was killed the day before the fort surrendered. The 1st Gurkhas had 'The Malaun Regiment' as part of their full title. (Mrs Madhu Gurung)

This shows how thick the walls were – virtually impregnable. The amount of effort to build such walls was incredible. (Buddhiman Gurung)

The Wedding

The bride is carried on the back of a male family member from her transport to her new family's house in Pokhara. Her hands are decorated with *mehendi*. The procession had come from Kathmandu. (Prem Gurung)

As she enters the house she has to snuff out five candles set in flour. Thousands of years ago Ram's bride, Sita, did this: 'if my feet burn it will show that I am not pure.' The bride's feet were unharmed. (Prem Gurung)

The Wedding

Family gathering. To the bride's left are her mother-in-law, Bhimkumari Gurung, and her father-in-law, Buddhiman Gurung. (Prem Gurung)

Bride and groom. The author enlisted the bride's father into 2 GR in January 1978. (Prem Gurung)

The author, who was OC of the British Gurkha Pokhara camp at the time, and HRH The Prince of Wales. (*Daily Telegraph*, 12 December 1980)

The author giving HRH Prince Harry a *Daily Telegraph* cutting, dated 12 December 1980, showing HRH Prince Charles leaning on a stick during his trek that finished the day before his visit to the camp. The heading, 'Prince Wants Bacon on Trek', was wrong. Prince Harry asked me if I wanted it back. 'No,' I said. 'Give it to your father for a giggle.' (Captain P. Lambert)

Lecturing New Recruits

The author lecturing new recruits in Pokhara on 27 December 2015, before their oath-taking parade. Here I am aged 90. (Author's collection)

The author inspecting the rear rank of recruits on 3 January 2016, shortly before they swore their military oath of allegiance. (Author's collection)

Home and Leisure Activities

On the roof of John's home in Pokhara. Behind is the Annapuna range of the Himalayas. Over John's head is the sacred mountain Machhapuchchhre, or Fishtail. Climbers are not allowed on this mountain. (Frederick Hudson)

Betty and Freddy Hudson with John Cross at the opening match of the Inter-School Basketball League 2011 in Pokhara. (Frederick Hudson)

What, no left-handed clubs? (Frederick Hudson)

The author and Buddhiman starting the first 5km in the local Pokhara Marathon, the former not helped by tunnel vision and uneven ground. There were no other nonagenarian entries. (Pramila Gurung)

On Getting Citizenship

Left: One of the staff of Tiger Mountain Pokhara Lodge traditionally felicitating the author on becoming a Nepalese citizen. (Marcus Cotton)

Below: Marcus Cotton and his staff at Tiger Mountain Pokhara Lodge with the author after the felicitation ceremony. (Tiger Mountain Pokhara Lodge staff)

On Getting Citizenship

735 people came to the open house to congratulate me five days after my citizenship was announced; many others told me they were sorry they could attend. Almost all of the guests that turned up had with them a present of a hat, a scarf or some other small remembrance. The local newpaper took this during the party. (Author's collection)

The author blessing one of his extended family during Dashera 2014. (Marcus Cotton)

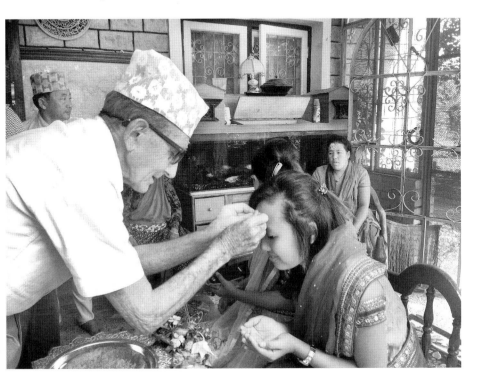

200th Anniversary Celebrations by 7th Duke of Edinburgh's Own Gurkha Rifles, Dharan, East Napal, March 2015

The author joined 1/7 GR when British Gurkhas started here on 1 January 1948. Here he is with Captain (QGO) Indrabahadur Limbu, a year older than he and a friend since 1948. On the right is Brigadier David Morgan, a friend since 1960. A whole raft of one-time British officers had come from the UK, Australia and New Zealand for a wonderful and never-to-be-repeated get-together with Gurkhas from Hong Kong, the UK and Nepal. (Rajesh Sakya)

The author addressing the audience, in English and Nepali. Two pairs of glasses are needed: readers over long-distance tunnel vision ones. (Rajesh Sakya)

200th Anniversary of the Raising of 1st Battalion, 1st Gorkha Rifles, 22–24 March 2015

Before partition, spring 1947. The author, age 21, and a jemadar platoon commander, both of 1/1 GR, resting on a road-opening day, North-West Frontier Province, India. (Author's collection)

The author, the only British person in the celebrations marking the 200th anniversary of the raising of the 1/1 GR, talking with Lieutenant General Ravi Thodge, colonel of the Regiment. The battalion was in Pathankote. (Buddhiman Gurung)

200th Anniversary of the Raising of 1st Battalion, 1st Gorkha Rifles, 22–24 March 2015

The author talking with the Subedar Major, 1/1 GR, Jaibahadur Saru. (Buddhiman Gurung)

The author talking with the Pipe Major, 1/1 GR. (Buddhiman Gurung)

200th Anniversary of the Raising of 1st Battalion, 1st Gorkha Rifles, 22–24 March 2015

On the way back to Nepal: the author patiently waiting eight hours at Lucknow Railway station for the onward train. (Buddhiman Gurung)

The Family Memorial

Father and son at the
memorial of their being
together for twenty-five years.
It was religiously dedicated
and is in their garden in
Pokhara. (Both author's
collection)

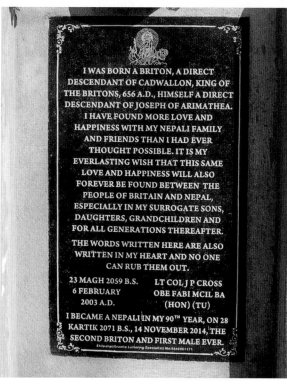

I WAS BORN A BRITON, A DIRECT
DESCENDANT OF CADWALLON, KING OF
THE BRITONS, 656 A.D., HIMSELF A DIRECT
DESCENDANT OF JOSEPH OF ARIMATHEA.
I HAVE FOUND MORE LOVE AND
HAPPINESS WITH MY NEPALI FAMILY
AND FRIENDS THAN I HAD EVER
THOUGHT POSSIBLE. IT IS MY
EVERLASTING WISH THAT THIS SAME
LOVE AND HAPPINESS WILL ALSO
FOREVER BE FOUND BETWEEN THE
PEOPLE OF BRITAIN AND NEPAL,
ESPECIALLY IN MY SURROGATE SONS,
DAUGHTERS, GRANDCHILDREN AND
FOR ALL GENERATIONS THEREAFTER.

THE WORDS WRITTEN HERE ARE ALSO
WRITTEN IN MY HEART AND NO ONE
CAN RUB THEM OUT.

23 MAGH 2059 B.S.   LT COL J P CROSS
6 FEBRUARY   OBE FABI MCIL BA
2003 A.D.   (HON) (TU)

I BECAME A NEPALI IN MY 90TH YEAR, ON 28
KARTIK 2071 B.S., 14 NOVEMBER 2014, THE
SECOND BRITON AND FIRST MALE EVER.

the butter into the shallow cups and the chant became louder and louder, then faded. The soldier was told to light the lamps and this he did, his hand trembling. Again the chanting began, low, subdued and formless. It gradually rose to a crescendo and, in startling and horrific cacophony, the instruments suddenly added their discordant threnody to the ululating voices of the lamas while the sightless, staring eyes of the Buddhas watched, blind and impassive. The stranger shuddered and was startled when large pea-sized grains of maize were suddenly thrown at the altar both by lamas and soldier. Then there was quiet and tension slowly unwound. Buttered tea was brought in and offered to all five men. Then it was all over.

An hour later they were gone, once more on the move. That night they camped in a cow byre near a frozen stream in the forest. The stranger then remembered that he had not entered up his diary since before leaving the soldier's house, so he searched for it among his few belongings. And although he was warm as he sat by the log fire, he again shuddered when he realised that he had just been spending Christmas Day.

2: Hope

The visitor asked the doctor in charge of the leper settlement how many Gurkha patients there were. Ten were being treated as outpatients, he was told, but one man was in a ward. His disease had not been diagnosed as contagious, nor was he disfigured in any way, but he was so disheartened that there was no hope of recovery. Death would take one or maybe two years to make up its mind. When it did, its prize would only be a pitifully wasted body.

The doctor took the visitor into the ward, having warned him to touch nothing. The ward held twenty beds, all occupied. In one corner was a bed with screens on two sides, shielding the occupant from the rest of the inmates. The visitor saw an elderly Chinese man, with ugly red weals on his back, sitting cross-legged on his bed, staring fixedly ahead. He seemed impervious to all that was going on around him.

The Gurkha lay in the middle of a line of deformity. Noseless, fingerless and hollow-legged humanity stared with apathy at the fit men, then smiled when they recognised the doctor. At the Gurkha's bedside the doctor called him softly, 'Here's a visitor to talk with you.' The sick man brought his eyes into focus and gazed with utter uninterest at the visitor, who turned to the doctor and said, 'Do you mind if I talk to him alone?'

'Please do,' said the doctor, 'as often and as long as you like. Excuse me, I have work to do elsewhere. You can sit down on that chair near his bed but,' he added solemnly, 'touch nothing.'

He turned to leave but, as an afterthought, turned back and said, 'Please do not talk to the Chinese behind the screen. He is serving a life sentence of solitary confinement for murdering his wife, who was also a leper. He is here only because this ward is emptier than any of the others.'

The visitor sat down and started talking to the lacklustre, listless Gurkha. Gentle prodding and sympathetic probing brought answers to his questions. The pathetically obvious yearning for compassionate comforting was as fervid as the reciprocal hope to inspire self-confidence. Half an hour passed and the man was tiring. The visitor got up to go, as he was also tired, having given some of himself.

'Listen, Gajendré, I'm coming back next week. You said you had not seen anyone for months, nor eaten for a long time. I can remedy the former, only you can remedy the latter.'

Next week the visitor was greeted with a smile. The remains of a meal testified the return of an appetite. Animation was evident and conversation lasted for an hour. Towards the end of his stay the visitor saw the sick man gaining strength as he himself felt correspondingly tired as his own strength was sapped once more.

'Gajendré, you're getting better. Keep trying. Next week you'll be sitting up.'

A week later Gajendré was indeed sitting up, the week following he was walking to the lavatory, and the week after that, on his fifth visit, the visitor had to go to the outpatients' quarters to meet him. Radiantly happy, although still very weak, he seemed well on the way to total recovery.

It was not long afterwards that there was an open day at the settlement. All was bedecked with bunting and the inmates wore new clothes. Just before the visitors' race, the visitor went and sought out the doctor.

'Tell me, doctor,' he queried anxiously, 'Gajindra Bahadur. How would you now describe his condition?'

'Miraculous.'

3:Charity

It was part of the traveller's charter to visit longhouses in the border areas of Sarawak and Sabah. In the course of a year he had walked many hundreds of miles and had, virtually, walked the whole inhabited frontier, visiting some places more than once.

One day he was told to visit a lonely house near the border. Troops stated to be already there would further brief him. He had with him a young Dyak policeman, who was serving his probation. Their route lay four hours parallel to the border along a rough track, mostly through secondary jungle. They walked through two security forces' ambushes. As it was most probable that the soldiers in the ambushes had not been forewarned, it can only have been luck that prevented fire from being opened. Not only the fear of more ambushes, nor the fear of the enemy, but also the shrill and incessant chirping of the small birds that allegedly predict rain made the journey nerve-racking.

They reached their destination around noon. They sat outside on the long veranda and asked for the headman. Women and children and dogs took no notice of the two men but someone must have delivered their message because shortly afterwards an agitated headman arrived. With scant ceremony he hustled both men upstairs into the loft.

'I have reports of enemy coming. You must hide,' he said.

The loft was airless and musty. The two men sat on the hard wooden floor and asked for details. After all, rumours were many, but the troops were nearby, so why the worry?

'Tell me, headman, where are the troops?'

'Tuan, they left this morning … you are on your own … the enemy are on their way … you must hide.'

So the long afternoon was whiled away in desultory conversation. Four times men came with news of an imminent incursion and all were unaware of the others' reports. The traveller had no means of communicating back to base so asked if he could go and warn the nearest troops, four hours and two ambushes away. The headman reiterated the necessity of remaining unseen. As a guest, albeit unwanted and unexpected, the traveller had little option but to do as bid.

'What do the enemy want here?' he asked. 'Have they ever said?'

'They are looking for Europeans, government men and border scouts,' said the headman in reply. As the traveller was all three he felt he probably qualified as a worthwhile target. 'They also want to shoot down a helicopter,' the headman added.

After sundown the traveller and his Dyak companion were invited downstairs for a meal of rice and vegetable. Neither professed to having much of an appetite.

As an enemy move against the longhouse was expected, it was decided to shelter the two men in a shallow grave-like pit dug under the headman's room. It had been dug for one man, now it was to hold two. There was no room for the men's packs, which were hidden elsewhere. Weapons would be carried, but firing them from under the stilt-perched house at night was adjudged too risky a business. However, weapons would most certainly be needed if evasive action became necessary. This pit had been dug directly below a 'trap door'.

This was part of the bamboo-slatted floor that could be rolled back when needs be. A man would put his sleeping mat thereon once the traveller and the Dyak were safely hidden. He would act as a decoy for it was hoped the enemy would not suspect anyone sleeping under any such rickety structure. It was decided not to get into the pit until absolutely necessary. Soon after it was dark the lamps were blown out and, no sooner had the traveller taken off his jungle boots, than the dogs up the track started barking urgently. 'Quickly hide. The enemy are coming,' the headman said.

In the dark the traveller fumbled with the laces of his boots. 'Oh hurry, hurry,' said the Dyak in agitation. 'Hurry, hurry,' echoed the decoy. The two men groped their way to the opening of the now rolled back bamboo slats, dropped a few feet and squeezed themselves into the narrow hole in the ground. As they tried to make themselves comfortable, the man lying directly above them urged silence. 'Quietly, quietly,' he hissed down at them, a vibrant urgency in his muted whisper.

The traveller had taken a towel down with him to use as a pillow. Within a very short time both men were beset by rats so the towel was wedged between head and wall and draped over his eyes. This manoeuvre caused the two men, already jammed together, to wriggle excessively. The Dyak gave little whimpers of fear as the rats ran up and down him. His tossings caused the earthen walls to start crumbling and all this drew more agonised requests for silence from above. The longhouse dogs were barking now, not the canine yapping at the moon, but suspicious man-induced yapping. The enemy was coming down the track.

Down below it smelt fetid. Under any longhouse human waste, pigs, curs, rats and fowls each leave distinctive smells. The traveller reckoned that, however uncomfortable it might be, sleep was essential, if only to help pass the time away. Much later he was awoken by a large rat sitting on his face. The constant movement of the rats over him probably aided by subconsciously trying to shake his head free, had resulted in the rats pulling the towel down and leaving his face exposed. He blew up at the rat and shook his head vigorously. The rat scampered off and somehow he freed one hand to drape himself once more.

It was a long night.

Next morning, at dawn, the two men were called up from their hole. The Dyak looked relieved. 'I never thought I'd see daylight again,' he said. The traveller looked less sanguine, but said nothing. They were taken straight up to the loft once more. By then it was raining heavily. Within half an hour three men had come in with separate reports that a large number of enemy had penetrated the area during the night, skirted the longhouse and gone deeper into Sarawak. They had come in at least two groups. Some were bearded. The owner of the dogs that first started barking had spent the night in the crude hut that was used during harvesting to save going to and from the main house, thinking it safer under the circumstances. The traveller felt that he should try to get his news back as quickly as possible. It was now urgent. His request to leave was politely refused.

'This rain has so swollen the two rivers that join below our house that you cannot cross them,' explained the headman.

There was nothing to be done. Men and children came up to the loft and huddled in a tight circle around the traveller and the Dyak. The local school did not open that day nor did the pepper pickers venture forth to their smallholdings. The traveller suddenly felt the onset of early morning nature.

'Oh, headman. I am ashamed. I must go and relieve myself,' he called down from the attic.

'This I forbid. Wait,' came the voice from below.

Within a minute the headman appeared carrying a red, handleless pot which he put on the floor in the very centre of the small crowd. The ensuing problems made the traveller forget the enemy threat.

The rain continued. A morning meal was offered and accepted, so as not to give offence. Both men merely picked at it. The Dyak, whose face had portrayed happiness on leaving the earthen hide, now registered deep gloom. On each report of the enemy being brought in, the difficulty of the situation struck the traveller more and more forcibly – the border to the south, up to 100 enemy to the north. The routes out of the longhouse were severely limited because of the swollen rivers. A ten-hour walk to the nearest soldiers if the enemy had only gone to the place the two men had come from the previous day. But what if the enemy had split?

The morning dragged on. About midday the rain stopped, but the rivers remained very full. During the course of the morning the traveller had found an old religious poster. It had four pictures painted in garish colours. The first picture showed a man, obviously a sinner because of the black looks emanating from his face, being chased by a tiger. The artist had very cleverly given a Mephistophelian grin to the tiger so no would-be convert need over-tax his imagination as to the allusion. The man was obviously about to get caught because a chasm and thick jungle completely blocked any escape route. The second scene depicted the man kneeling in prayer, the tiger gathering itself for a spring that would ensure both its own dinner and the man's demise. However, fresh developments were shown in the third picture. An exclamation mark, dropped by a European-looking angel, hung conveniently over the desperate man's head. The tiger looked nonplussed. In the fourth picture the exclamation mark had even more conveniently turned into a stepladder and the man, now a firm believer in the faith, made the more obvious by the smirk on the angel's face, was climbing nimbly up it. The tiger was slinking disconsolately away, his face turned round with a vexed expression caused by the unusual and unpredictable way his quarry had eluded him.

Both the traveller and the Dyak wondered if there was a moral to the story.

Once more the headman was asked if he would allow the traveller to leave. The urgency of informing somebody about this incursion grew steadily. The answer was definite. 'Please do not go as long as there are enemy in this area. If they were to know I had hidden you, they would punish me with my life. This is their real threat.'

At 2 p.m., twenty-six hours after they had arrived at the longhouse, they heard a helicopter. There was an agonising wait to make sure it was in fact coming their way, followed by an exquisite feeling of relief when it circled the longhouse. It had obviously come for the two men but equally obviously it had not heard of the incursion.

The two men ran to the small field 200 yards away and the traveller marshalled it to the ground. He flung his kit and weapon in, pushed the Dyak in, climbed up the side and lifted up the surprised pilot's helmet. He put his mouth near the pilot's ear and bawled, 'Hurry, there are over a hundred enemy nearby and they have threatened to shoot the first helicopter they can. You are the first since the incursion.'

The pilot waited just long enough to allow the traveller to get into the body of the machine and took off faster than he had landed. There were tears in the traveller's eyes not accounted for by the wind as he was sitting sheltered from it.

Some months later the traveller returned to Borneo and was told that a broadcast by the enemy radio had demoted him two ranks and announced his death. This had also been reported in the local daily paper the following day.

The traveller's battalion pandit (from the days when he did not have to travel quite so much) was smiling when they next met.

'We say that if a man is reported dead yet stays alive, he will live till he is a 100 years old. You have had two reports about you. This means that you can now be with us till you're a 110.'

The Dangers of Gossip

'Habits up in the village take a long time to change,' my Nepali friend told me. 'Time is slower there than elsewhere, I sometimes think.'

I was well aware of the Nepali characteristic of an elephantine memory. I have been reminded of events of more than a score of years earlier being brought out as though they had happened just the other day. We had been talking about the situation as it was developing here in Nepal in March 1994, with rumours about a vote of no confidence in the prime minister.

'There have always been bouts of political turbulence of one sort or another, especially in Kathmandu, but locally also. I can so well remember talking about one particular incident that I had just heard about. I was about 10 years old.' Now in his late 30s, that would put the date at around 1958. I knew his village was Thuloswara, in western Lamjung, not far from the border with Kaski. It is a large place covering the side of a mountain. A quick walker, travelling light and starting very early, can reach the snow line of the inner–Himalayan range within the day.

'I had just heard of some trouble between us and another tribe from the north. That night I asked my father if he could tell me more about it. Before he had time to open his mouth – well, he had opened it but he had a stutter – mother bade me keep quiet. "You must never talk about those times, son. It is very dangerous to gossip. Many of our menfolk spend too much time gossiping. You never know when those who shouldn't hear will hear and get angry again." So I kept quiet but I will tell you what I know. It had happened some time before ...'

My mind went back to the troubles in the early 1950s when the Rana regime had been toppled and the Shah dynasty, virtually eclipsed since the Kot Massacre of 1846, came into its own again, as it had since Nepal was unified under King Prithvi Narayan Shah, in 1768. In fact, the Shah dynasty can be dated from 1559 when Gorkha was captured by Drabya Shah. From 1949 to 1951 I had been instructing in the Army School of Education (Gurkha) in Singapore and, during the troubles, students recently returned from their home leave in the east of the country told me of an Indian-domiciled Nepali congressman, Deoprakash Rai, leading an armed band from Darjeeling into Nepal as far as Ilam. This man had been a colour sergeant instructor under me and I had temporarily to take over his Nepali teaching practices when he left us in a hurry – sedition, attempted conspiracy with the communist enemy and attempted mutiny. He had died, a campus folk hero, not long before I joined the staff of the university in Kathmandu in 1982.

In 1967, when on trek in the east of Nepal I was shown bullet holes in houses that had been shot up fifteen or so years before. There had been many such shootings in other parts of the country that I only heard about later. The army of Nepal was busily engaged and, in 1994, I found one old soldier who took part against the agitators and who still remembers it all very vividly.

The story continued: 'Our people were being harassed from the north and, in desperation, they sent a delegation to the strongest family in Syangja to help them.'

I understood that both parties to the unrest were hill men, strongly represented in the Indian and British Armies as 'traditional martial classes'.

'From Syangja town?' I queried.

'No, from Nawakot, the old defensive fort just over the Kaski–Syangja border.'

That puzzled me until I remembered that, very often, clandestine groups worked away from administrative centres – Trisuli used to be the base for dissatisfied elements from Kathmandu.

'How long it took to persuade the head of family, Kulamandan Shah, for help is uncertain. Eventually his grown-up second boy, called Kalu, went back with the delegation as the community's leader. I expect he was accompanied by a wife, servants, if not retainers, as were all important people in feudal days.'

The son having a different caste from his father puzzled me. I had enlisted Khans and Sahis myself, but not Shahs. Also, all periods of the Rana regime were known as 'feudal' but I had not realised that part of the Shah family still lived around Syangja. Not wishing to show my ignorance, I kept quiet.

'Up at the top end of our village is a large stone, called the *Sinduré dhuñga*, which had been used in past times for kings to be crowned. That was during the period of the 22 Raj and the 24 Raj. Lamjung was then a separate entity. This is where Kalu was officially recognised as the paramount person in the district.

'Six months after he got there, he went north, up the Marsyangdi river, to liaise with the folk upstream but they ambushed him and his two companions. They were tied to trees, shot and killed by a man called Banjharé.'

Banjharé was a name I had not come across before. As far as such violence was concerned, I remembered the first British visitor in that area, Major T.J.W. Allen, telling me that when he was there, in 1950 I think it was, he was threatened by people carrying firearms. I mentioned that and got a surprising answer.

'They were killed by arrows, not shotguns.'

I wondered why; was there a shortage of cartridges or had possession of the others been illegal, smuggled over from India, so not talked about? Who was to know? 'Weren't people very angry? How is it that I haven't heard people talking about it?'

'I'm telling you. We eventually got our own back on them. Parleyed with them on the banks of the River Marsyangdi. They got drunk; we didn't. We won. The prisoners we caught had to continue life in a very much more lowly caste than either group. Some of them migrated to western Syangja, 50 miles away over the mountains. None of us talk about it. That was what my mother had said to me. We children were not to gossip. It is dangerous to talk about it, so we don't.'

I let that pass. I was intrigued in how long it took to fix a return match, so to speak, so I asked. My friend was not sure, but maybe it had been about ten years later.

I did a calculation. That meant the action took place in, say, 1961. I had heard nothing about it. Just as well, I supposed, that the Western media had not got wind of it; otherwise the human rights angle could have been embarrassing.

'After Kalu was killed what happened?' I asked.

Apparently another delegation had been sent to the same family, still in Nawakot, to get another of their sons. 'Pushing their luck', was my unspoken comment.

'The mother was most loath to give another of her children, although she had many, seven in all, Kalu being the second. Eventually the Lamjung villagers prevailed and they were taken up to where the other children were sleeping, all together under the same blanket. One, the youngest, had crawled above the pillow and was by himself at the head of the bed. "We'd like him," the leader of the delegation said. He was only 7 years old and had to be carried back up to Lamjung. His name was Yasobam.'

That was another name I had not come across before. Again, not wishing to show my ignorance, I kept quiet.

A pause.

'When he came of age he was married in the village.'

This threw me. 'How long after his arrival would that have been? If he was only 7 when he arrived there, surely that was much too early for any marriage?'

Times were vague, only the place was in no doubt. Then there was a son born, so that gave me a clue. Say, at the earliest, the father was 17 at the time, which would have put his arrival up in Lamjung earlier than I had been thinking. Ten years earlier? That would make the date around 1940. I don't like interrupting so I kept my thoughts to myself.

'The son was given the name of Narahari and grew up in the area. He became the chief after his father died.'

I was really lost now. The timings were awry. I tried to work it out to myself. The narrator's father was, I knew, born in 1931. His wife was a few years younger but any trouble that had been of a serious nature would still linger in people's conversations when she was young. She would remember it well enough to tell her son not to talk about it.

'What happened then?' I asked after a pause.

'Oh, Narahari Shah stayed on in Lamjung but his younger brother went over to Gorkha to make his mark there.'

'What was the name of the younger brother?'

'Drabya Shah.'

'But, surely, Drabya Shah was the founder of the present royal family 1559?' I cried out in disbelief, so muddled by now that I had to show my ignorance.

'Yes, that's the one I am telling you about,' came the patient reply.

A quick mental calculation, my mind in a whirl: 'That would put the delegation to Nawakot in around 1493! That's over 500 years ago!' I burst out.

A sigh; a smile. 'Yes, my mother is very afraid the other people will get angry if we start talking about that time. Those we managed to beat might take it into their heads to do something in return. She still says it's very dangerous to gossip.'

Two Royal Visits to British Gurkhas, Pokhara

1980 and 2016

Before Prince Harry's visit to British Gurkhas Pokhara on 22 March 2016 he had intimated that he would like to meet anyone who had been there when his father visited the camp on 10 December 1980. I was the officer commanding/deputy recruiting officer (west) then and my surrogate son and my eyes, Buddhiman Gurung, had also met him and shaken his hand ('Oh, how soft it was!'), so we both qualified. I remember the visit well.

Piloting his own plane, closely monitored by the squadron leader pilot, Prince Charles arrived at Pokhara airfield exactly on time. I was there but kept out of sight as I was fixing his blood (someone had to be *in situ* wherever he went), the first secretary's return flight and the defence attaché's clothes.

The prince went on a few days' trek, during which time he pondered heavily on family affairs, before visiting our camp.

Before the prince arrived with us I stood in the middle of the assembled throng and, loudly, briefed the many 'old and bold' there to meet him that I would escort Prince Charles and, behind me, the British ambassador would escort Prince Dhirendra. As I was virtually blind each man had to introduce himself to His Royal Highness. Outside the guardroom the guard waited to give the royal salute and outside the mess three soldiers waited to unfurl the Union flag, HRH's standard and the Nepalese flag.

The royal motorcade drove into the camp. 'Here they come,' said the ambassador.

'Which car is the prince in?' I queried, seeing only a blur.

'The one with the flag on, you fool,' came the caustic answer. The convoy stopped in front of the mess. I went to open the door of the leading vehicle and, only just in time, realised that I was about to open the chauffeur's door, not the prince's. The ambassador presented me and I, having saluted, shook the proffered royal hand.

'Welcome to the British Gurkha Centre, Pokhara, Your Royal Highness. I hope you enjoyed your trek!' I presented the Gurkha major to him and the Gurkha major's wife garlanded him.

In the mess the prince turned to me and sternly said, 'I don't like Pokhara – unfriendly and dirty.'

I gave no answer and only later learnt that from 3 a.m. the police had had to obliterate a lot of offensive graffiti on many walls between the prince's hotel, Fishtail Lodge, and the camp. Nepalese not British royalty was unpopular and one way of expressing dislike of it was to put Prince Charles' name instead.

We moved to the table by the window and I offered him a drink – squash. He gave me a signed photo of himself for the mess. 'Put it where you like and throw custard at it after a mess night.' I gurgled a polite laugh. He surprised me by saying, 'I hear you speak nine Asian languages and you need to buy more land.' We had a desultory conversation while he drank his squash and, before going outside, I asked him to sign the visitors' book. Concentrating on him as I was, I took no notice of what the ambassador and the Nepalese prince were doing: I let my second-in-command, Captain John Rogers, help them out where necessary. Fearing to be accused of lèse-majesté, I refrained from mentioning to the Prince of Wales that my own pedigree – direct descendant of Cadwallon, King of the Britons in 676; of Cynwyn, Prince of Powys; of the wife of Llewellyn, the last Welsh Prince of Wales killed by Edward I between 1282 and 1284 – made me nearer the Welsh throne of antiquity than the prince.

Once outside, to a clicking and flashing of cameras, we started our 'talking walk'. I presented Lieutenant Colonel Alastair Langlands: 'Colonel Langlands introduced Her Majesty to the ex-servicemen twenty years ago, Sir!' In the first group were three holders of the Victoria Cross, one of the George Cross, as many of those members of the Royal Victorian Order (5th Class) who had been Queen's Gurkha orderly officers as the prince grew up as we could, those holding an honorary rank and a 3 GR honorary captain, Birtasing Gurung, one of only two Burma War fighters given a Soviet Union decoration (the other was a lieutenant colonel in a British Battalion). I presented each man in turn. One of the three holders of the cross was Tulbahadur Pun. Earlier, on his way down to Pokhara he was knocked off a precipice by a boulder. He was unconscious for two days in great pain and coughing blood. He continued on down to Pokhara, half carried, half walking, with six broken ribs, a broken shoulder bone and a pierced lung. By all odds he should have died. HRH was vastly impressed that he had made such an effort to come and see him.

In a wheelchair was Naik Nandalal Thapa, 8 GR, who had won the Empire Gallantry Medal (later upgraded to the George Cross) for rescue work during the Quetta earthquake of 1935. 'I rescued twelve men but the citation only put ten!' he shrilled. 'Poor old man,' the prince said, 'still worrying about it nearly fifty years later!' After presenting those especially invited, we moved along the line, starting with the dhobis, the Indian canteen contractor, other civilians and on to our ex-servicemen.

The prince put out his hand to be shaken by one old man who remained stock still, his visage stern and almost bellicose. The prince's empty hand flapped. 'Shake it,' I said to the old man. 'I don't know how to,' came the surprising answer. 'Try,' I told him and shake it limply he did. 'What is your regiment?' the prince asked him. 'I'm a civilian. Never a soldier,' he answered curtly. 'Why are you here?' 'To see you. It took three days to get here. With one day here and three days back that's seven days' field work lost.' He had wormed his way into the camp. The prince was visibly touched. Five or six media merchants behind us, one of them a woman, softly guffawed. Later she would write that the old man was a holder of the Victoria Cross.

'There are an awful lot more, aren't there,' the prince said, looking round as we moved on. 'Bear with it, Sir,' I said. 'It may be hard work for you but it's a day in a lifetime for them.' My Gurkha major came up to be and whispered, 'You're behind schedule.' 'Top gear, Sir, we've got to get a move on.' Quicker. A few minutes later came another furtive whisper from the Gurkha major: 'Too fast!' 'We've got to move more slowly, Sir.' All the while there was a mixture of friendly informality and interest. And exactly to the minute we finished on time. The cars started up and drove to the pick-up point.

The prince turned to me: 'How long have you been here? How long have you got? What will you do afterwards?'

I answered his questions: 'Just over four years; just under eighteen months; I have no idea.'

'Then I'll have to find you a job.' His last remark was intriguing and mysterious. The future king? Surely he's not one to have throwaway words like that? Yet what could he mean? I put the remark into the hibernation of my memory bank and was grateful for his concern.

There were many plaudits from all concerned as they left. I was pleased that I had not let my almost complete blindness show. Back in the mess, a cup of tea had seldom tasted better.

Not long afterwards I got a letter from my mother in which was a *Daily Telegraph* cutting from its 12 December 1980 issue about Charles on trek, with a picture of him leaning on a stick. The caption was 'Prince Charles Wants Bacon On Trek.' She asked me if it was true. I found out that it was, in fact, a member of his party who hankered after pig meat. There were two other mistakes: I corrected them in ink on the top and the side, sent the cutting back and forgot about it.

I asked the (then) Lieutenant Colonel Peter Duffel, a friend of the prince, if he could follow up his invitation. The prince's private secretary, the Hon. Adeane, had not heard the prince talking to me so declined to take it further. However, being asked was of great use: in 1984, I wrote to King Birendra asking to be allowed to stay on in Nepal. In my letter was a paragraph about being asked to work for the future British king. I saw a photostat copy of the letter: that paragraph had a 'goose's egg' round it whereas the others only a vertical line in the margin.

★★★

Fast forward to 2016: two days before Prince Harry's visit I was rummaging in a drawer looking for something to do with Malaya when, lo and behold, I found that amended cutting! I was sure Prince Harry would be interested so I took it to the camp with me. I also thought that he would be interested in two of my books, *Gurkhas at War* and *Gurkha Tales*. 'Will Your Royal Highness accept two books?'

'Yes.'

In both I had written: 'Your Royal Highness Captain Harry Wales, Humbly, with Affection and Admiration.' Buddhiman had signed the former and I had signed and dated both.

I showed the prince the cutting and explained it. 'Do you want it back?'

'No, give it to your father for a giggle.'

When he opened *Gurkhas at War* and saw Buddhiman's name and signature he turned and made *namaste* to him, to Buddhiman's intense pride and delight. The cover of *Gurkha Tales*, with the Himalayas as background, especially pleased Prince Harry. 'I am lecturing the new recruits,' I said. He opened the book and there was a photo of all the recruits and their staff from Gurkha Company, laughing.

'They're not doing any work. They're laughing.'

'Yes, at my lecture.'

'How long have you been with Gurkhas?' he asked.

'Seventy-one years, three months and twelve days.'

'That's a long time,' he said with a surprised look on his face.

And my last words were, 'Your Royal Highness, the tie I'm wearing is that of the regiment that bore your great-great-grandfather's name, the 1st King George V's Own Gurkha Rifles.' At that he showed great interest.

As he passed Buddhiman, standing on my left, he again made *namaste* and said, 'Buddhiman, look after the colonel.'

Ears to the Ground

'Really, it is not what you hear but what you think you hear that makes a person react in a certain way. I could give you a sad example of a man who started imagining voices calling him and so acted very strangely. These voices urged him to run away into the jungle with a loaded rifle and during the subsequent hunt for him I found him lying in a patch of long grass. I had an anxious few minutes waiting for him to decide if he was going to shoot me. Luckily he was overpowered before his mind had been made up.'

The young men listened to the pensioner, wondering why he had decided not to go on with a story that sounded gruesome but they were ready to listen to whatever he told them. 'It is when your eyes cannot reach out very far into the undergrowth that your ears have to take over. In the jungle I can remember a patrol that surrounded what was thought to be some enemy making a camp and talking, only to find an unusual combination of a pair of woodpeckers pecking holes in a tree, a group of monkeys with sticks hitting branches not so far away and a river that gurgled over stones in such a way that the leading scout reported voices. I happened to be on that patrol,' smiled the pensioner, 'and our senses were all directed towards the bandits making that sort of noise so naturally that is what we first thought the noises we heard meant. Rather like when there's a newborn baby in the house – even a mouse squeaking makes the mother think it is the baby needing attention, or when one is waiting for an airdrop and has to put up smoke as soon as the aeroplane is heard to start putting green leaves on the smouldering fire just because one of those noisy beetles is flying about out of sight nearby.

'Having felt a bit foolish when we realised we had been surrounding monkeys and woodpeckers we did not want to be caught out another time. One day I was out on a patrol with three others, Dhojbir, Mohansing and Phistabahadur. We were travelling very light, weapons and ammunition only, without even a water bottle. We only expected to be out for the best part of four hours. Going down a slope we heard what I took to be the noise of someone hoeing. Now hoeing does not make all that much of a noise and one of the others whispered that it was a pig rubbing its back on a fallen log. It did cross my mind to ask him if it were a pig why whisper so softly but I remembered in time that we were never meant to raise our voices unless shouting out orders during an attack. We moved cautiously forward, just in case it was not a pig – and it was not! It was a bandit cultivation, fenced in, and had many fallen trees lying around. At the far end there were two men hoeing; the noise was loud because that patch of ground was harder than most.

'"We'll creep in and take up a fire position by that fallen tree," I ordered and led the way forward. We crossed over the fence and crawled out into the open, out of sight of the two men in the far corner. We felt dreadfully exposed, especially as we were used to the dark protection of the canopy. It was strange to be crawling because, however much you learn as a recruit, the times that you have to crawl seem few and far between. By the time we had gained the fallen tree we were panting with our exertions.

'"We'll catch our breath and then Mohansing and I will take on the lower of the two men, and Dhojbir and Phistabahadur the other men,"

I ordered. I waited what seemed an age and then gave the order to fire. I had one of those carbines, light to carry but not much stopping power.

'I must leave the story for a short while to tell you that, over the past month or so, I had been haunted by a dream – a nightmare to be accurate. I was in contact with the enemy and I fired at one man but my bullet had no effect on him as the safety catch of my weapon always managed to put itself on before I fired. Then the man would turn round and fire at me, killing me but somehow so that I did not die but only awoke in hospital. It was a monochrome dream, black at the edges and white up top. So vivid was the dream, which haunted me as I said, that I especially asked if I could test my weapon on the range – and in my excitement I did forget to release the safety catch. Any rate, I thought I'd laid the jinx. But back to the cultivation.

'"Ready?" I asked the three men. Yes, they were ready. So I took careful aim and saw that, such was the angle that the man on the left – my target – was bent over, I could not aim at his head. I thought a couple of bullets in his back would suffice so I squeezed the trigger and hit him where I had aimed. He swung round with his hand behind him and, keeping the same aim, I squeezed the trigger again. And, just as it had been in my dream, nothing happened – and monochrome: dark jungle and white sky. In a flash I tried to pull back the working parts but, desperate though I was in my hurry to knock down my target, I could not move the wretched thing. I was baffled.

'In cold blood I know it sounds stupid now, but so real was the effect of the dream that I instinctively pinched myself to see if I was awake or not. In that split second the others, not the brightest of fellows, thought I had been wounded and concentrated on me and not on their target. I saw which way things were going, and which way the two bandits had started going also, so I ordered a charge with the traditional battle cry, "*Ayo Gorkhali*, Charge". We rose from behind our tree trunk, I clutching my useless weapon, just as the two bandits disappeared from sight. So the two men escaped but one of them left his rifle behind. Thinking that someone might come and collect it, I decided to send back two of our group and to keep one man with me and we would wait all night if necessary and ambush the rifle. I thought that the platoon commander might want to come up to us that evening and continue tracking the two men if there was time. In the event he did not come until the following morning. The one man who stayed with me was the only non-smoker and he could more easily bear the smokeless night.

'It was only 4 o'clock when the other two left us alone. We decided to keep in the cover of the jungle overlooking the rifle and not risk going to find water although we were very thirsty. We found an anthill that we could take a fire position behind and, tensed, we waited until it was dark. We decided that one of us should be able to doze off for half the night and the other to keep awake and change roles around midnight. At about eight o'clock we both heard a low grumbling sound. "What's that, do you think," I whispered to Mohansing.

'"I think it's the bandit you hit laughing," he replied.

'"Why on earth should he laugh?" I queried in amazement.

'"Only because the Gurkhas' bullets have not been able to kill him and he's happy."

'I felt it was highly unlikely that it was a man laughing. Far rather it was the wretched fellow I had shot and what we had heard – and then again – was the death rattle in the hapless man's throat. That was my theory and I stuck to it although Mohansing preferred his version. Be that as it may, it was one of the longest nights I can remember.

'I was alert for an attempt to regain the jettisoned weapon but visibility, already limited, disappeared when it started to rain. I was also wondering what the platoon commander would have to say to me on the morrow. Before it had become fully dark I had banged my weapon heavily on the ground with my hand depressing the working parts and, at last, I had managed to open the breach. The spent cartridge had swollen to such a size on its being fired that normal force could not move it. I kept the spent cartridge as evidence.

'Around midnight, when it was my turn to doze off, I was scared out of my wits by a gentle and plaintive snickering noise that I could not identify for sure. It was castrato treble and I also heard the undergrowth being moved. I shook Mohansing who, like all our countrymen, had God's gift of being able to fall asleep under the most adverse of situations.

'"What's that?" I asked him when I'd woken him up. The noise had not been heard again since I'd shaken him so how could he know? "Mouse deer," he said, referring to the smallest animal of that kind there is.

'Ages later the dawn came. We were both hungry and thirsty but we stayed where we were until the rest of the platoon arrived around 8 o'clock. We then emerged. Recriminations were kept till later, certainly while the area was being searched. There was a maze of tracks showing that the bandits were in strength somewhere albeit not in the immediate vicinity. I went to see if the corpse was still there. It had to be, for how could anyone have come and taken it away during the night? But it wasn't anywhere at all. If I had killed the man he certainly hadn't died there.

'Did someone ask what was the laughter or the rattle we heard? Yes, I'm coming on to that, but I still feel a bit ashamed when I think of it. No, it wasn't a man at all. We only thought we had heard one because no other noise fitted what we were expecting. It was a tiger. There were big pugmarks. Its scent drifted downwind and that is why we didn't smell it. The mouse deer would come in and nibble the new produce in the bandits' cultivation and the tiger was waiting for its supper.

'I think you'll agree we all, on both sides, had a lucky escape that time. It's not that we can't hear so much as we don't know how to listen.

'Did someone say "Hear, hear"?'

The Gurkha Independent
Parachute Company vs
Indonesian Infiltrators

In June 1966, reports in Borneo began to be heard that a man called Sumbi, a person feared by the local people, was training about 100 volunteers in jungle warfare, over in Kalimantan, and boasting that, one day, he and his men would cross the border and march to Brunei Bay and thereafter sabotage the Shell oil installation in Seria. The rumours persisted. Then, on 23 July, a report reached Ba Kelalan in the 5th Division of Sarawak, that Sumbi with some fifty men, had moved out of Long Bawang, in Kalimantan, for 'an unknown destination'.

The battalion opposite Sumbi's probable crossing point was 1/7 GR. It was thought that Sumbi would try to infiltrate between Ba Kelalan and Long Semado, over a lonely, high and cold, jungle-covered ridge. Patrols were sent out to try to locate any movement. In front of these battalion patrols were men from the Gurkha Para. Two men of one patrol, Corporal Jitbahadur Rai, and Rifleman Dharmalal Rai, were out on 29 July, early in the morning on a reconnaissance near the border. Dharmalal saw something on the jungle floor glint. He took no notice of it – many things with a speck of dew on them glint in the morning sun, but, on their way back, approaching from the other direction, he spotted it again. Curious, because had it been dew it would have dried out long before, he examined it. It turned out to be a small piece of foil, smelling of coffee. Coffee was not a feature of Gurkha rations; British troops might, for all he knew, have coffee in theirs, but there were no British troops within miles. It therefore had to be Indonesians; but there were no tracks.

The two Gurkhas cast around a while and did discover tracks for two or three men – but the tracks were of British Army jungle boots, making as though from the border northwards into Sarawak, so the two men decided to return to the three others (of that five-man patrol) and follow the jungle boots. This they did.

There followed an extraordinarily patient and expert piece of tracking. From midday on 29 July through to the 31, these five men slowly and inexorably tracked the footprints. For two nights they did not make camp or cook anything, fearing that the noise and the smell might give them away. It is very cold at night in the Borneo uplands.

On the third day their patience was rewarded: they found not only the three pairs of jungle boots but sacking – to tie round the feet so as not to leave any distinguishable marks – for more than forty-five people. How right they were not to have relaxed their precautions. Having established that their quarry had indeed continued northwards only a short time before, they opened their set and gave a full report to their tactical commander, the CO of 1/7 GR, and to Para Company HQ.

Initially the report was scarcely believed by 1/7 GR (and I, the company commander, was particularly angry) so, to make doubly certain, the Gurkha Para patrol was sent to backtrack the footprints to ensure that they had come from over the border and that this group therefore had to be Sumbi's.

From then on 1/7 GR took over the tracking of Sumbi and this gang and, from the first contact until the final incident when Sumbi was captured on 3 September, which was after the official end of confrontation, many troops were deployed, including a company of 2/6 GR, three platoons of Police Field Force, a platoon of Border Scouts and five more patrols of Gurkha Para. It was a very complicated and well-planned follow-up; tracks were found, followed up, then lost, then found again – numerous times. The country was extremely rugged and radio communications became difficult to maintain, so control was never easy. Some of the raiders were captured, some surrendered and some died of starvation. By dint of tight planning, clever debriefing and flexible deployment, success was achieved, all but four men being accounted for. The threat to Brunei's oil supplies was no more.

Towards the end of the chase the country was viler than it had been; after two weeks of cliff hanging, river crossing and slow tracking, twenty-four enemy were eliminated. 1/7 GR could account for forty-six eliminations. The officer who eventually captured Sumbi at the very top of a precipitous feature, Major A.M. Jenkins, of 1/7 Gurkha Rifles, was awarded the MC. His Gurkha captain who was with him was aggrieved to learn that he, the QGO, had only been awarded a 'C' grading on a jungle warfare course at the British Army Jungle Warfare School yet Sumbi, who had also been a student there as a lieutenant in the Indonesian Army, had been awarded a 'B' grading.

When, on 7 December, *The Times* published an account of the Sumbi incursion, it was with the headline 'Courage of the Gurkhas Foiled Saboteurs' and it continued 'Details of one of the most brilliant actions in the history of Gurkhas have just been released ...' and went on to describe Rifleman Dharmalal Rai's meticulous attention to detail as he sniffed the tinfoil that smelt of coffee.

After the confrontation was officially over, everyone in Malaysia – Sarawak and Sabah – had to stay in camp, waiting for orders for the peacetime pullout. We, in the Gurkha Para Company, were not in Malaysia, but in Brunei, so these ceasefire orders did not apply, so we were still operational. The Brunei government wanted to know if the last four of Sumbi's gang had, in fact, infiltrated into Brunei or had died in the Sarawak jungle. In an area of wild country that could have been anything from 500 to 2,500 square miles, the odds against finding men were infinitely remote. Nevertheless, a patrol was sent to the border of Brunei and Sarawak, a ridge of hilly jungle, to see what it could pick up. One of the soldiers, Rifleman Jamansing Rai, needed evacuating and, with the pressure of other duties relieved, I flew in to take his place.

Corporal Chandrabahadur Rai put me as no. 4 in his patrol and off we went along the border ridge. The jungle was dark and damp. It had been raining. We travelled slowly, keeping our eyes peeled. And then I saw it – a leaf, one of myriads in all that vast expanse of jungle, caught my eye because it had an unnatural crease, making its outline straight. Man must have done this, yet we were the only people in the area. There was just a chance that it was Sumbi's last found men. I called Chandrabahadur's attention to it and we cast around even more thoroughly.

Our search revealed more suspicious signs, moving away from our area into the Royal Brunei Malay Regiment's area on our flank. A message was sent to them, alerting them as to the possibility of trespassers.

I got a message the next night from the CO, an old friend of mine who had spent all his life till then with Gurkhas. 'Why?' I was asked, are you frightening my soldiers by pretending to be a ghost?'

Working, as we were, on Morse code prevented me from sending a fitting retort. All I could do was to send a 'Wilco, Out' and leave it at that until I emerged from the jungle and went and saw my friend.

This I did; the Brunei soldiers knew I was on their flank. The day we found the leaf they had sent a party to get water from a stream in order to cook their evening meal. Approaching a thick bush a voice, speaking in English, ordered them to stop, turn round and go away. This they had done and, on reflection, reported that a ghost had spoken to them; otherwise how could a voice, disembodied and unexpected, be anything else?

Their CO knew better but, still unconvinced that the evidence we had found was correct, presumed that I had tracked the prints of some local Ibans into his company's area and, out of sheer impishness, pretended I was ethereal.

In fact, four men did emerge from the jungle, from the direction where we had been patrolling and, almost dead from starvation, went to an Iban longhouse in the valley below and asked for food. As they were eating, the soldiers fetched and captured them. They indeed were the last of Sumbi's gang and, at their interrogation, one of them did admit that he did have a habit of plucking leaves, folding them and then discarding them, as well as being a twig breaker.

Would those four men still have been captured had one of them not had 'restless fingers'?

Onomastics and Teknonymy

Onomastics: the study of proper names, especially of their origins; teknonymy: having a parent named after a child or a child named after a degraded person or object. 'So what?' as the sewing machine asked the nudist. I thought I'd spell out one or two nuggets I have picked up over the years to which a reader might like to add – or from which to subtract!

Taking onomastics first, it may come as a surprise to learn that maybe more than 99.99 per cent of all Nepalis never use or even know their correct name. This means that every Gurkha soldier who has enlisted since 1815 has likewise given a 'false' name to him who recorded it. This is because the true name, his *rashi nam*, 'zodiac name', which could more meaningfully be rendered as 'soul name', once given at birth, is virtually never mentioned again so that evil influences cannot use it to enter the person when, or if, others call him or her by it. The southern Irish are also inclined to take this precaution.

That means that any other name used is 'flexible' and, virtually, a nickname, only permanent once that has been accepted after the pundit has told the head of family with what letter the name to be used should start, and then the infant's family. And even then it can be changed at the whim of its owner. Buddhists work similarly. My second surrogate son's accepted name was Hombahadur. When he completed his proof of citizenship document he entered his name as Haribahadur. 'Why,' I asked him, 'did you change it?'

'Because I liked it better,' was his answer. Such 'flexibility' has been the bane of countless record officers and the bewilderment of many impoverished widows when discrepancies over names occur – as they do neverendingly.

There is a plethora of other nicknames, some pejorative, such as 'snot nose', 'bandy legs', 'round eyes' and 'midnight' for a dozy individual, and others more descriptive: 'third son from the other side of the lake', 'tal pari saiñla'. Others are merely polite: 'elder brother', 'cousin brother', 'grandfather' and 'uncle', and their female equivalents, and others of that ilk. That means that many people do not know either their father's or their mother's name. Nor do many know when they were born. However, a clue can be got from the name the person goes under: the name of the week becomes the first part of their name. For instance, a man born on Monday will be *Som*-something, *bahadur* or *lal* for example, and for a Friday, *Sukra*-something, *raj* for instance.

Now to castes. I have a theory (and I am in a minority of about one here) that the traditional *jats* (castes) were, originally, nicknames. Below the *jats* that we all recognise, and which have often been changed for recruiting reasons, come *thars*, immutable sub-castes, clans or tribes (depending on which dictionary you use). The 'old' Indian Army had a handbook of all *thar* and sub-*thar* of all its soldiers, a fascinating document. The British Army, in its wisdom, has never felt the need for such a publication. Reasons for *jat* nicknames are, I believe (and here I have to admit that my knowledge has yet to become all-embracing), were intimately associated with *Bahuns*, hill Brahmans, 'plains men' Brahmans being *Jhas*. Even one of their sub-castes, *Lamichhané*, derived from *Lamo Kan* (long ears) is found in both groups. *Guruko añg* (limb of the guru) is a near enough rendering. *Thapa*, found both with Chhetris and Magars, is part of the verb 'to set up', 'establish', namely *prasTHAPAna garnu*. *Rai* is a historic Hindu accolade for, I think, bravery. *Limbu* I know not: *Yakthumba* is their own tongue; its own script was lost but found during King Mahendra's reign by a Scotsman and Parasmani Pradhan, a Darjeeling linguist, when hunting in the British Library. Both were honoured by the king. As an aside and nothing to do with names, the race of people with the closest DNA to the Limbus are the Tonkinese of North Vietnam. 'Chhetri', *Ksatri*, as well as *Rana* – not a normal 'n' but one Romanised with a dot – have connotations with the battlefield.

In turn you have Sens from *sena* (an army), Mallas from *malla* (a wrestler) and Tamang from the Cantonese *ta* to fight and *ma*, a horse. When I was in Tamang country I witnessed their annual festival day: surrounded by men waving one arm, as though holding a sword or pike, a man in the middle, wearing a bandolier, had a model horse's head tied near his navel and the tail from the base of his spine. In English the *ma* root is found in 'mare', a female horse, and a 'marshal', a horse-bound commander, be he field marshal or earl marshal. Once the communists had taken over Laos, all the dancing consisted of the arm-punching fist-waving variety, so sadly different from the graceful, curvaceous loveliness of traditional Lao dancing.

'Khan' comes from when the animist Genghis (by one spelling) Khan was supreme. After conquering most of the then-known world, it was self-preserving flattery for both Muslims and Hindus to say they too were Khans, of the 'leader's' clan.

Shrestha and Pradhan – 'first' and 'foremost' – are Newar tribes, related to *Nepa*, the Newari for Nepal. *Thakur*, a leader, has its roots with *thekadar*, a contractor.

Whether Magar really is *ma gar* (*chhu*), 'I will do it', is still doubtful though some claim it as such.

Duras, the clan that started off as Turas, and was thus in the language, were famous during the time of the Anglo-Nepalese War, or rather before. The famous Bhakti Thapa was a Dura and only changed his *jat* and became an honorary *Thapa* so that snobbish seniors would work under him. In the Nepali *Nepal's Military History*, produced for King Birendra, Bhakti Thapa is the only commander whose family history is not given correctly. I know because I was asked to vet the 666-page book for the chief of army staff. Incidentally, Bhakti Thapa's weapons are still worshipped every Dashera, spring and autumn, and a pig is sacrificed on both occasions – Duras are the only people who sacrifice pigs at Dashera – and the prayer leaders still use the Dura language (although calling it by another name): there is only one Dura speaker left alive, an octogenarian widow.

Strangely, after the Gorkhali government was defeated in 1816, the name 'Tura' or 'Dura' seemed to vanish, although I have come across just a very few so names. Duras chiefly enlisted as Gurungs: old lineage records have them listed as 'Dura Gurung' and even 'Dura Thapa'. When I started writing my historical novels in the mid 1990s, the Indian Army did not enlist Duras because they were not on any Nepal government list of Nepali tribes, castes or clans: by the time my vol. 4 was published, the Indian Army had begun to enlist them.

The Yadavs found in the Terai are members of the Yadu family to which the god Krishna belonged.

Enough of *jats*: now briefly on to place names. 'Kathmandu' meaning 'wooden temple' and 'Pokhara', 'lake', are well known. The study of Nepalese place names, of any country's come to that, is worthy of a master's degree. Most large rivers in Nepal end in -*di*, the Magar for 'water'. This gives me the feeling that that is another strong indication that the Magars came over the Himal prior to other epicanthic eye-lidded people. Two that always please me are in Laos (that name still shrouded in mystery): the River Mekong – *Me*, mother, *Kong* river – it, until recently the longest unbridged river in the world and the world's thirteen longest, and Vientiane, not *Vien ti ane* but *Vieng* 'a fortified town' and *Chan* from *chandra* moon, so 'fortified town [in a bend of a river] in the shape of a half-moon'. The French always made guttural, throat-clearing noises with 'ch' sounds so the *chan* had to be spelt with a 'ti' (like the 'ti' in 'attention', and the English, not knowing why the word was spelt thus – and why should they? – had their own pronunciation that no Laotian recognised!

From 257 to 208 BC, the earliest date we have, 'Vietnam', as it is now known, was Au Lac when the Chinese moved into it and changed the name to Nam Viet: *nam*, 'south' and *Viet*, the Romanised ideogram for 'getting somewhere with difficulty'. After eight more changes in name, in 1792 or 1802, from Dai Viet as it was then known, a delegation went to Peking ('northern capital') to ask for the old name of Nam Viet to be restored. The emperor said that to keep the name given by the Chinese would only mean that they, the Chinese, would feel they had to return. To prevent that he would allow the name but rendered backwards, thus 'Viet nam'.

Borneo and Brunei are different spellings of the same word and 'Gurkha' is an English word. *Hukum*, an order, in fact really meant 'royal command' and since Nepal's monarchy was dispensed with the word too has become redundant: *adesh* is now 'order'.

Bahadur, brave, as a name has fallen out of fashion. The only place to find a remnant of it is the capital of Mongolia: *Ulan*, red; *Bator*, hero – now spelled as one word, Ulaanbaator.

So, a short word on Teknonymy: all those who have served with Gurkhas will know that a wife will call her husband '[first born's] father', never by the name others know him. The degraded person habit is now dying out but it explains why especially Gurungs, once known as *Kami*, blacksmith, *Sunar*, goldsmith or *Sarki*, cobbler, are all now *dalits*, or even *Kalu*, for black; colour consciousness is still a large factor of Nepali life. Strange, indeed, how fair-skinned people like to be photographed looking tanned, while darker-skinned people prefer overdeveloped photos that make them look paler than they actually are.

As for degraded objects, I quote the Mara of Mizoram in Assam: if the eldest son dies, any son born thereafter is named something like 'cow dung', 'pig shit' or 'dog shit'. All right, you can quote back at me some of the sessions of the Australian Labour Party in their Parliament!

Here endeth the second lesson – 'not before time', I hear in the background.

Names

Names, a universal commodity mostly taken for granted, come in many guises, from the simple and nondescript, through the slightly ridiculous to the majestic and jaw-achingly difficult – and all so easy to forget or get wrong!

Take, for example, three simple ones, Cross, Organ and Slim. It is chiefly in puns that they are used: 'Oh, another little Cross to bear?' to an expectant mother; in the case of the late Derek Organ – 'How lucky to have a name like Organ when in charge of a one-man band!' said the chief instructor of the chronically under-staffed Jungle Warfare School to British students; and, during that battle in Burma, over the field telephone to a harassed adjutant, 'It's the Thin Man here, coming for lunch.' The frustrated and unbelieving answer, 'And this is the … Gas, Light and Coke Company,' was not forgotten when the 'Thin Man', General Slim, arrived in person.

Having the surname Cross can be particularly difficult. Twice my name has been badly misconstrued when thought to refer to the highest decoration for valour: once in Kathmandu in 1947 and the second time, in the same place, three and a half decades later. They bear retelling.

I and a friend were touring the mint, bear-led by a Rana lieutenant colonel whose English was only as good as would be expected. No paper money was in general use, only coins, and a sack was needed to carry any sum more than a few pence. When introduced as Lieutenant Cross, the man in charge had understood that I was a holder of the Victoria Cross. On bidding farewell, he took my friend's hand, shook it cursorily before he started lauding me on being such a special man: could he have a copy of my photograph? Would I be here at the next *durbar*? When was I returning to the plains? And many other questions. He was so embarrassed when he learnt of his mistake that, throwing down my hand, which he had been shaking for quite some time, he turned and walked smartly away leaving us to find our own way out of the building.

The second time was when I was being filmed for the American programme *60 Minutes*. 'Just one more question, Colonel. When did you get your Victoria Cross?'

'It's not Victoria it's John, so a sex-change and renaming ...'

'Cut!'

Gurkhas, bless them, no longer find foreign names quite so difficult as they used to: longer and more complex names were almost always slaughtered by them. The ones I remember best are; Lord Louis Mountbatten, 'Mountain Battery'; General Festing, 'Mess Tin'; General Sir Nigel Poett, 'Niggle Pot'; Lieutenant Colonel Vaughan, 'Bhagwan'; and Major Tedford, 'Tailboard' – and I am sure you may be able to quote countless others. It somehow lessens the owners' status when their names are mangled but it can work the other way. During the Malayan Emergency an admittedly brave and clever bandit, Tan Fook Leong, was made to sound bigger than he was in real life when his name became Ten Foot Long.

Our soldiers have always been cavalier with names, spreading from the two facts of only the never-used 'soul' name being the one that really matters so rendering other names as less important – and how many record officers have torn their hair at another misnamed soldier leaving his widow pensionless? – and the constant use of inter-family names. And, of course, there are nicknames, which even extend to animals. On the North-West Frontier of (then) India, two of our thirty-nine mules had nicknames. One, the idlest, was called the Brigadier as no one had ever seen either do any work, the other the Quartermaster because neither would let the local hair clipper anywhere near them!

When I was trying to get through American Immigration in 1959, I told the official that USA and UK military had a lot in common. 'There's NATO,' I told him.

'Never met General Nato, but he must be good to give his name to that lot,' was the only answer I got for my pains.

I don't suppose that there has ever been a General or even a Mr Nato but giving surnames to places can have a happy outcome, as one of the national newspapers told us in 1953 when the eponymously named Mount Everest was conquered for the first time. 'Ever, Everer, Everest' is a fortunate combination for the world's highest mountain but how sad it would have been if Sir George Snodgrass or Sir Erb Buggins, for instance, had been surveyor general of India at the time – although Sir George did insist his name be pronounced 'Eve-rest'. At least I was not as brash as my French counterpart when I was in Laos: I overheard him telling someone that *Pancha Shila* (the five moral precepts of Buddhism) was the name of a high Buddhist monk in Tibet. Well, it might have been, mightn't it? I told him later.

At one time I thought I was good at remembering names but, ever since an incident when I was a young officer, I have had a mental blockage, certainly as far as women are concerned. So badly that, years later, I called the CO's lady by the name of the second-in-command's wife's godparent, who had helped at her baptism. I was icily told that I was muddling her up with her enemy. 'Don't ever call me by that dreadful woman's name again,' I was admonished, 'or you'll be my enemy for life.' Not even a bouquet of flowers made up for that one. Time had to be the great healer!

But the blockage started with such a bizarre incident that I have to say before anyone reads it that it is, in fact, true. And it happened like this:

At the first Brigade of Gurkhas annual conference in Kuala Lumpur, some time back in early 1949, I, a subaltern, was detailed as GSO3 Dogsbody. That was the conference at which it was decided that we would have all-Sandhurst-Gurkha-officered battalions by 1975, and at which the newly formed Gurkha Scout Troop sang their one and only English song: 'Sweetly sings the donkey/At the break of day'. A delegation of interested staff officers were to fly up from Singapore to attend. They were due to spend two nights in the HQ camp which, you must understand, boasted two messes. My job was to receive the officers as they arrived on the scene and direct their baggage to whichever mess they had been allocated. Simple. They were late and the first session of the conference had started by the time they arrived.

I saw them get out of their coach, one of the rare ones that was not being used for children's school runs. They were agitated and in a hurry. 'Don't worry about your luggage,' I said to them. 'I'll get it all sent up to the messes and it'll be in your room when you get there.' I knew from a list that I had been given who was to be put where. They seemed relieved to let me get on with that chore and save them a journey that would have made them later still. They disappeared into the large Nissen hut that did for a conference hall.

I looked at the baggage, checked my list of where who was to go and got it into two piles, one for A Mess and the other for B Mess. A vehicle had been laid on and the kit was loaded up and delivered safely to the mess staffs. On the programme there was, so I had noticed, half an hour's mid-morning break in the proceedings and, just in case I was wanted, I went back to the place where the officers had de-bussed. This was on a road junction with an uphill road going to each mess, both 200 yards away. During the coffee break everything seemed quiet so I thought I could dismiss and take my fatigue party back to the unit lines. As I was gathering my men together, I happened to look up and I saw one of the staff officers coming down the road with a suitcase. He was red-faced and sweating.

'I thought you were going to get the kit into the right mess for us,' he said querulously.

I still had the list in my pocket. 'May I know your name, sir?' I asked. 'Jones. Major Jones. I thought you knew.'

I ignored the unreasonableness of the remark and looked at the case he had put on the ground and I saw that Jones was the name on it. There was only one Jones on the list. I was on the point of mentioning that I could see no reason for his upset, politely of course, when I saw another of the staff officers coming down the other road carrying yet another suitcases. He, too, was red-faced and sweating and was also a major.

'I thought you were going to get the kit into the right mess for us,' he said querulously. I looked at his case and saw the name was Smith on it.

'Your name, sir?' I asked.

'Smith, Major Smith. I thought you knew me.' My military discipline kept me from making the reply I felt the situation deserved. Also there was only one Smith on the list.

Majors Jones and Smith then noticed the suitcase that the other had carried down the hill. 'That's mine,' they said in unison and took possession of the case that the other had brought with him. I was amazed to see Major Jones take the case with Smith written on it and Major Smith take the case with Jones written on it. I could not believe my eyes. What pantomime were they practising for?

Luckily the vehicle that had come for us was commandeered for their suitcases and their owners to go back up the hill to A Mess and back down and up to B Mess. When the vehicle came back the second time I simply had to find out where I had gone wrong. Jones is Jones and Smith is Smith, or so they had been up to then.

I saluted as the officers got out of the vehicle in order to rejoin the conference that was on the point of restarting. 'Excuse me, sir, but could you tell me where I went wrong in thinking that Jones was Jones

and Smith was Smith and Smith is not Jones and Jones is not Smith?'
It was all a bit of a mouthful but I managed somehow.

They both looked embarrassed. It appeared that both Smith and
Jones had recently married. Major Smith's wife's maiden name was
Jones and Major Jones' wife had been Smith. How was I to know that
each of the two officers had taken their new wives' suitcase, which
still had their old names on when they came on the conference? That,
surely, is in the realm of mind reading! It taught me never to take what
I see at face value, try to react to the unexpected and to stand up and
be counted.

All that so threw me that I immediately muddled up two highly
decorated senior officers – at least five Distinguished Service Orders
(DSOs) between them and goodness knew how many other honours
– who were at the same conference because their nicknames were, in a
way, similar. I had to send envelopes containing some important papers
to both of them and, being me, of course I got it wrong. I sent the
one that should have gone to Brigadier 'Deadly' H★dl★y to Lieutenant
Colonel 'Killer' V★ck★rs. Too easy when a person is muddled, and
'deadly' and 'killer' have much in common – especially in this case
when I sampled the wrath of them both. But I never did let on why
I made the mistake!

But as I've already mentioned, it was women's names that constantly
floored me. The incident with the colonel's lady may have started it,
and not mentioning women's names in the mess may have continued it,
but I fared badly when, on one longer leave, I tried to get married. She
was a nice girl, daughter of a youngish widow and I thought I popped
the question most stylishly. She was sitting down so I got to one knee,
took her hand and asked her to marry me. I forget how long I had
known her but I was due back to my battalion fairly quickly. I recall I
even called her 'darling'.

Unfortunately she was a stickler for protocol. 'Why don't you use my
name?' she asked irrationally – she obviously had no sense of humour.
I didn't reply but used the 'darling' word again.

A 'look' came into her eyes and she struggled to sit in the upright position. 'You don't know my name, that's what it is,' she accused me.

'Of course I do,' I glibly lied, having completely forgotten it, using the 'd' word for a third time.

The wretched woman then called my bluff. 'What is it? I won't answer your proposal until you tell me my name.'

Put that way, it was tantamount to the ball being in my court. I hazarded a guess, vaguely remembering a name I'd heard used in her presence. A look of scorn crossed her face. 'That is my mother's name. You've got the wrong woman. You're not the one for me, nor I for you. No. Never!' was her devastating reply.

I must, however, count my blessings: I suppose we were both spared a fate worse than death. Both? Yes, only us two. I crept out of the house before her mother heard she might be the one up for grabs. (Forty-five years later, a middle-aged lady came on trek to Pokhara. She enquired if a Colonel Cross was there. She was my 'misfire's' daughter!)

Surnames that are used as first names almost always floor me. I have the greatest difficulty if the fellow is, say, Duncan George or George Duncan. Once on the telephone I thought I'd got it right but when I was accused of being 'very Victorian today' I knew I'd failed again.

In 1953, still very much in the not-so-palmy days of sea trooping between Singapore and Calcutta, I sat at the chief engineer's table with two others, one Tony Cronk of the Gurkha Sappers and the other a Belgian lady of indeterminate years, a Madame Bippe. I well remember that first meal together. In the broadest of Scottish accents, the chief engineer asked us our names. His eyes opened wider and wider and he burst out with a roar of laughter, 'Oh dearr, dearr, Cross, Cronk and Bippe. Never before and never again!'

Once we reached Calcutta, customs confiscated a soldier's (albeit legitimately brought in) gold. It fell to me to recover it from customs, having obtained the authority from the Reserve Bank of India. It took two days finding my way through a frustrating bureaucratic maze but at last I was successful. All I needed on the third morning was a signature from the head of department, an aloof looking individual by the name of Bugga. I said, 'Good morning, Mr Bugga,' but, the chief engineer's laughter still rankling, did not ask after his family – no more than a talking point, you'll agree – as it might not have sounded too good if I had asked after his wife and all the little Buggas. But I did get the man's gold!

Names, names, names …

Giving of Myself

In a newsletter obituary we had described how a certain officer had shown considerable courage in disarming a murderer: 'A QGO, a weak character promoted above his ceiling, ran amok with a kukri. He killed a fellow QGO ...' In his obituary it would have been inapposite to have mentioned that the murderer then tried to commit suicide and the final outcome of the tragedy. I don't think these have ever been mentioned in any of our newsletters. Let me remedy that.

I, in 1/7 GR, came on the scene shortly after the murder: it was late 1952 (so the murderer and murdered were King's not Queen's Gurkha Officers) and we were in Seremban. I was planning to go on a trek with the late Major Jimmy Marks, later Macdonald, 1/10 GR. Being the first time ever that any British officers had been allowed to go on trek – not advised to go separately – we were wildly excited. Our proposed route was from Darjeeling to Kathmandu.

I was given the background and told to go to the local hospital, where the King's Gurkha Officer (KGO) had been brought for treatment, as interpreter for a legal team charging him with murder. This I did. The charged man took no notice of any of the proceedings.

I continued planning the trek but was told we would have to wait until the accused was put on trial because I would be needed as witness to the fact that he had been charged with murder. The trek was postponed and we were unable to rearrange it. (When I was the attaché in Laos in 1972, the head of chancery told me that he had first 'heard about' Nepal in connection with Jimmy's and my trek. His department had disallowed it. 'Why?' I asked. 'Because it was new and might have caused difficulties we were not wanting,' was his candid answer.)

The wounded officer got better and was transferred to Sungei Besi, where 2/7 GR were, and kept under close arrest. He would not talk to anyone, including the Gurkha major and the 'Trick Cyclist'. He was almost, if not entirely, cataleptic. I was sent for. 'Go and talk to him. Get him to tell you what happened.'

It turned out to be easier said than done. I went to his room, dismissed the sentry to for the next ninety minutes tried to get him to talk. He was entirely indifferent and did not react in any way. I felt as if I was talking to an immobile zombie. Admitting failure and not wanting to waste any more time, I left him and went back to the mess for a bite. I told the CO that I would return to Seremban, some 42 miles to the south, as I had failed dismally. 'Go back and try once more.'

This I did and, dismissing the sentry once more, made my final effort. I leant towards the man, slumped in his chair and oblivious to all around him, willing him to talk. I tried to push something from deep inside me out towards and into him in an effort to bore into his mind, hoping to arouse him. He started to perk up. I continued trying to push, willing him to catch hold of my 'it' – whatever 'it' was – as I got weaker all the while. The more I pushed the harder he pulled and, sucking me almost dry, he suddenly sat bolt upright. Animated, and in a clear, steady but weak voice, he told me why he had done what he had.

'After I was commissioned I was laughed at and bullied because I was not good at my new job. As a WO1 [warrant officer] I could manage but as a lieutenant I could not. I was driven to distraction and, having killed my main bully, tried to get rid of myself. I failed.' It seems that he had realised that he had, indeed, been over-promoted.

By then I was at the end of my tether, breathing shallowly. Not being able to give of myself any more, I pulled myself – but what part of me? – back inside. As I pulled, so he weakened. Once I was all inside myself he slumped forward, cataleptic once more. I dizzily stood up, called the sentry and tottered back to the main building. I told the CO what I had learnt and returned, fatigued, to Seremban.

I learnt that the man never spoke again.

I have managed to give of myself twice since, once saving the life of a Gurkha signalman who had contracted leprosy and had not had a proper meal for a year. The other time was to my fiancée, who later succumbed to cancer. Now, an old man, I daren't try again even if I could, which I don't want to.

Mind over Matter

There were at least six of us who had been hurt at one time or another, two when parachuting, the rest otherwise. Remedial treatment in conventional hands was slow, painful, time consuming and not always successful. The threat of the surgeon's knife with the ensuing pins and catgut was never far away. Once things became drastic enough for these measures, the end was in sight.

When I was told that a local Malay not only had the power of healing but was also willing to try it on me I was interested, albeit sceptical. Over the years I had heard of such men but had tended to disdain them. However, as with almost everything in life when a decision has to be made it is the alternative that gives the impetus, I asked if I could meet him. He was brought to my office the next Saturday morning, some two months after my parachuting accident. No man, it is said, is a hero to his butler. No man, I say, looked less like a healer than the small, gap-toothed, wizened little fellow who beamed his way chirpily into my office, clutching an old and very dirty trilby hat. Experience won over the years has made me chary of judging by first appearances so I just let matters develop naturally.

The man, Yasin by name, addressed me in a parody of fractured Malay that could only have been learnt from a Gurkha. He repeated the phrase *ini macham*, 'like this', as some Westerners will repeat 'you know' and 'sort of'; it clearly meant nothing. Yasin was, so I later learnt, the fourth generation of healers and had served as a special constable during the Emergency when he had escaped from a number of communist ambushes. Now he bade me strip and sit down. He next asked for a glass of water, most of which he threw away. He then placed it on a table, closed his eyes and started muttering incantations over it and occasionally blowing into it.

I strained my ears to catch what he was saying but all I heard was a vague '*nickety nickety*, blow, blow, blow, *maso maso maso*, blow, blow, blow, *hamla hamla hamla*'. Any esoteric meaning was lost but at one time I did think I heard him say 'Cross for prime minister' but I could have been mistaken. This pantomime continued for a couple of minutes and I was then ordered to drink the water and place the glass upside down on the table. Obediently this I did.

Yasin then set about prodding, pinching and generally exploring my shoulder. Diagnosis was then made. 'If you had seen me the day of your hurt,' he said, 'I would have cured you within a week. Now, only if the gods so wish and you have a clean heart, will I be able to help you get better. Even then it is quite possible I can do nothing for you.' Any feeling of elation I might have had at the end of the first session remained stillborn, encased in gloom. His parting shot was that he would come round to the mess that evening for my first spell of treatment.

Thus began an exercise in dichotomy as well as therapy: Yasin came to my room as often as he remembered and I went to the hospital as often as I was ordered. For the former, Yasin's brew had all the characteristics of an embryo cottage industry. It had a distinctively rural smell and it, too, had to be prayed over not only at the beginning of a session along with the water, but also at the end when he washed his hands. At the end of each period I would reward Yasin with a packet of cigarettes or a soft drink. As for my arm, I had been taken to the threshold of pain each time and both Yasin and myself would end up sweating. In sharp contrast, my conventional treatment was barren of action or drama.

Some four weeks after my secret treatment had begun I was threatened with an operation, medical opinion being that it were better I had limited, though unnatural, movement than be 'frozen' for life, as seemed the probable outcome. Yasin was most disturbed. This diagnosis was, he felt, the wrong one. Twice he had been proved right in his diagnoses by a subsequent X-ray after his magical fingertips had found why some areas were stubbornly not reacting to treatment. Now, in his opinion, eventual recovery was at stake. If Western medicine was to be drastic, Eastern medicine had to act quickly to forestall any irrevocable consequence. 'I will transfer your pain to a chicken,' he announced, 'and, if you have faith and a clean heart, you will get better.'

Next Saturday evening Yasin came into my room and asked me to provide, by early Sunday morning, the following: six Straits $10 bills, twelve 1-cent pieces, betel nut and lime, nutmeg, a clean handkerchief, a plate, a healthy chicken and five rust-free nails. I forbore to ask him if a partridge in a pear tree was also on the menu.

When all was ready, the glass with its inch of water, the chicken tied to the leg of the chair, on the edge of which a Gurkha corporal, dragged in as a witness, sat uneasily, Yasin, the high priest, started. Incantations and blowing were intense, and I felt that only a roll of drums was needed to add just that touch of panache to a scene that otherwise was starkly informal. The muttering rose to a crescendo and I distinctly heard 'Cross for prime minister' twice. Treatment began after I had set the glass upside down having drunk the water. The normal ritual was enhanced by Yasin eating the betel nut, lime and nutmeg, placing the handkerchief over the glass and pocketing the cash. I noticed that the five rust-free nails were untouched and wondered just what part they had to play. The chicken was then unwound from the chair, prayed over, blown over and its claw drawn down my bare shoulder three times, waved around my head three times and, likewise thrice, spat on by me.

Its beady eyes held a tinge of reproach and I felt somehow that events were overtaking it too quickly for its natural composure. However, it only remonstrated once and that was when it was banished to the mess lawn.

This marked the climax of the treatment. Yasin lay back in a chair, sweating profusely, obviously spent. The Gurkha excused himself and I was left contemplating five rust-free nails on the plate and one recumbent son of the soil.

Before Yasin left he told me that he would not see me for another three days, during which time he would take the chicken home and feed it properly, 'for,' he added with a touch of peasant concern, 'it would be wrong not to look after god's creatures'.

The next three days saw my shoulder as stubbornly immobile as ever: there was no sudden freedom of movement, no welcome release from the irksome restrictions the injury imposed. Maybe my heart was not clean enough – maybe I was not going to be prime minister after all.

Wednesday evening saw Yasin burst into my room, face aglow. The spell had started working: the chicken had until that morning behaved as any normal, self-respecting, healthy chicken should behave but suddenly, around midday, it had mysteriously developed a stiff right shoulder that had prevented normal movement and had caused it to go round and round in circles. Two hours later it gave up the struggle that had obviously and unfairly been unequal all along: my pain had been transferred to it and it had been unable to bear it. Four days later my arm started moving more freely and much less pain and within the month all was as it had been before.

The night before I went to see the specialist, Yasin said to me, 'Don't tell him I've helped you; let him think his own treatment worked,' which I thought was either very broad-minded of him or else remarkably prescient. At the medical interview I was put through a number of contortions. The specialist burst out laughing when he saw the effortless ease of it all. 'Excuse my French,' he said, 'but this is bloody wonderful. I had had no hopes that you would ever be fully fit again.'

I still do not know what Yasin does with his mounting total of rust-free nails.

Numbers

Soon after I started living as a civilian in Pokhara in 1986, a very old friend of mine and my ex-Paklihawa Gurkha major, Birkha Raj Gurung, came to see me. He was very keen that I be integrated into local society. He knew that my best defence against any whims of those who were still suspicious of my status was for me to be 'part of the furniture', accepted by all and sundry. He saw that I should approach the problem on two flanks, Hindu and Buddhist. I was very happy about this as, despite being a baptised Christian, I was aware that the local gods had as much need to know me and recognise me as friendly as I had need to be accepted by them. I saw no clash.

The Hindu aspect surfaced first. A new temple to the goddess Kali was to be installed in the local bazaar, to the south of Pokhara town, not far from the Indian government pension paying camp. Birkha Raj was the main organiser: land, money, shrine and goddess. He called in one morning and asked me to be at the stone-laying ceremony. He would be there also and would tell me what to do and where to do it.

I went as bid and sat at the back of the rows of chairs to one side of the large square stone *chautara* in front of which proceedings were to take place. I was called forward to sit with the senior guests. I saw that a subscription was inevitable and, mindful of living on a restricted budget while waiting for life assurances and an old age pension to mature, felt 1,000 rupees, worth about £30 then, would be about right. Birkha Raj, sitting next to me, asked how much I was willing to give. I sensed he was uneasy when I told him. He went away to register my amount and came back looking grim. Leaning over he quietly asked if I was sure I wanted to give 1,000 rupees. Knowing I would not be taken advantage of if I gave him the decision to make I asked him how much he felt I should give. The reply was unexpected: 1,001 rupees.

That incident set me thinking about the part numbers play in the religious or cultural fabric of any group. Having been aware of unlucky number 13 and the way hotel rooms and aircraft seats are numbered 12A, it had never struck me that odd numbers were more favourable to the Nepalis. On asking why, I found it is because odd numbers are seen as incoming to oneself and even ones going the other way. Merit, to be effective, needs to be directed towards oneself – indeed, the definition of religion that pleases me the most is 'conduct directed towards one's own salvation'. And does not charity begin at home?

I seem to remember being told, when still small, that even numbers for us in England were lucky but, thinking about the temple donation incident, I remembered being taught to blow dandelion seeds or pluck petals chanting 'she loves me, she loves me not', where the odd number appears to be the lucky one. I say 'appears' as it can never be taken for granted that love is a two-way phenomenon. Certainly 'three times lucky' is an old adage, and a third death is always to be expected after two have happened in quick succession, but where 'two is company, three is a crowd' three seems not to be lucky. As for being at sixes and sevens ...

In the Malayan Emergency there was a 2 in the date every time my company had a success when I was out with it, never on any other day. It was uncanny the way even the most obvious contact would go wrong if the 2 was missing.

Back to Nepal. A single *shri* is attached to any title to make it polite and I recalled the way to write letters when I first joined was to add three *shris* — *Swasti shri tin shri* ... for a normal polite start with the three being upgraded to a five for anyone seen to be of a higher social status — *Swasti shri panch shri*. Indeed, the prime minister during Rana times was known as the 'Three Government' while the royal family still holds the moniker the 'Five Government'. Recently, reading the history put out by the Royal Nepal Army, I was interested to see that the Malla kings of the sixteenth century had the courtesy title of only two *shris* — *Shri Shri*. Had the greater number, three, been introduced when the whole of Nepal was united in 1768? Reverting to the one-time letter-writing method, an even number, especially four, implied enmity not amity. Somewhat sadly I felt, 'two' was reserved for the wife, even though it implied the 'other half of the pair'?

I was fascinated years later to find a *shri* 107 for certain well-qualified priests who worshipped Ganesh. Among this select band within the subcontinent, two Nepalese names appear on the official list of merit. In parenthesis, *shri* also appears in names: a town, Shri Nagar (town); the capital of Ravana in Ceylon, now Shri Lanka; and, quite why I have yet to find out, in Muslim Negri Sembilan, Peninsular Malaysia, the village, Shri Menanti.

Numbers having a significance with religion appear to be as old as the hills, however old they happen to be. On glancing through *Brewer's Dictionary of Phrase and Fable* I see that Pythagoras looked on numbers as influential principles. The number 1 was unity, and represented deity, which has no parts; 2 was diversity, and therefore disorder: the principle of strife and all evil; 3 was perfect harmony, or the union of unity and diversity; and 4 was perfection, being the first square ($2 \times 2 = 4$). The prevailing number in nature and art was 5; 6 was justice; and 7 the climacteric number in all diseases.

In old Christian ecclesiastical symbolism, I further noted that 1 is the unity of God and, leaving 2 out, 3 is the Trinity. Each number up to 13 seems to have its special significance; 7 is particularly holy, with the

Seven Churches of Asia, the Seven Gifts of the Spirit, to say nothing of the Seven Deadly Sins. Seventh Heaven and Cloud Nine are obviously much later additions. The number $9 - 3 \times 3 -$ is especially holy. Sacred writing is full of groups of three words when, were the writing normal prose, two would be ample.

However, the people who really incorporated numbers or, rather, a numerical value into everything, were the Hebrews. Except for E, every letter had its value. Not being allowed to mention the name of the Almighty, whose real name, JHVW, in any case was unpronounceable, the next best only was allowed, Jehovah Adonis. This added up to 91. In religious ceremonies of ancient times many people at the fringes of meetings could not hear all that was being said, so to get 91 up to heaven all at once and at the same time and not to use the sacred name of the Almighty, the man in charge of the ceremony would raise a red flag so all could see and that would be the signal for the permitted 91: $A = 1, M = 40, E = 0$ and $N = 50 -$ thus 'Amen'. The name change from Saul to Paul resulted in the new name being nearer the mystic 91 than before. The number 40 has a meaning of indefiniteness rather than an exact time span, as forty years wandering for the Jews, forty days and forty nights in the wilderness.

It seems that 666 was a code number the Jews used against the Romans. A mystical number of unknown meaning, it refers to some man mentioned in the Book of Revelations and is based on the 'number of the beast'. One of the most plausible suggestions as to its origin and meaning is that it refers to Neron Cæsar, the infamous Nero to most people. Its numerical value in Hebrew characters gives 666. Since then 666 has been widely regarded as a very bad number and the act of beasting is to add up the letters of a person's name to 666. Someone worked out, but probably did not tell the man concerned, that if $A = 100, B = 101$ etc., the name Hitler adds up to 666.

The golden number of the Christian Church is any number between 1 and 19 and is arrived at by a complicated formula based on the Metonic cycle, itself composed of the awkward number of 235 months after which the phases of the moon recur on the same day of the month. It does not seem to have any connotation of luck by religious rectitude. In contrast, the Ten Commandments are basically easy to understand.

Another seemingly awkward, but very lucky, number is 729 or 3 × 3 × 3 × 3 × 3 × 3. The Greek philosopher Plato, who wrote the *Republic*, believed, perhaps surprisingly, that the very best form of government was to have a really good king: then, in descending order, Aristocracy (assuming that these few were good), Democracy – A (assuming these many were good), Democracy – B (assuming these many were bad), Oligarchy (assuming these few were bad) and Tyranny (assuming this one was bad). The marks given were that Monarchy was 729 times better than Tyranny. He did not spell out the intervening marks but Aristocracy perhaps scores 243, Democracy (good) 81, Democracy (bad) 27, Oligarchy 9 and Tyranny, not the 3 to be expected as being more logical, but only 1.

Many in the Western world do not take figures into consideration when grave affairs of state are involved. However, elsewhere this is not always the case. In 1973, the late Prince Souvanna Phouma, then prime minister of Laos, used his fixation with numbers, especially those that had some affinity with others, to decide on which day the ceasefire would take effect. He decided that 23 February was to be the date, when, two days before, such an event as a ceasefire seemed very remote. The war had been going on for twenty-three years, and 23 February was a coincidence too good to be missed. There was also the merit of 2 × 3 equalling 6, a figure divisible both by 2 and 3 with a happy answer of 3 and 2. Some saw the decision being motivated by a religious consideration rather than being prompted by mere superstition (where is the cynic who asks me what is the difference?). Whatever the root cause, at least a decision was made.

In Hindu Nepal, 3 has a special significance in religion, names and mystic symbolism, and I give examples of how the number appears in compounds. It is difficult to keep them apart as each aspect overlaps on to one or both of the others. Only a few religious concepts are straightforward: the trinity of Brahma, Vishnu and Shiva; the cities of gold, silver and iron in the sky, air and earth built for demons; and the chief three duties of a Brahman: sacrifice, study of the Vedas and giving of gifts or charity.

Two examples of numbers appearing in names are Tribhuvan or Trilok, the three worlds, used as an epithet for sacred Ganges, seen by Hindus as flowing through three worlds; and 'three-eyed' and having 'hair in three twists', epithets for Shiva.

Mystic symbolism embraces *Trisuli*, the three prongs, or teeth, the trident; an aggregate of worldly existence, religion, material goods and fulfilment of manhood; the triple subjection of the religious mendicant, of thought, word and deed, symbolised by carrying three long staves tied together to form one, the three states of loss, stability and increase; the three folds of skin about the navel of a woman, regarded as a mark of beauty; a law-suit in which a person engages from anger, covetousness or infatuation, a derangement of the three humours of the body and many more.

However, it is the number 5 that comes into its own, leaving the three designations I gave for 3 well behind. The coming together of five, or more, the *Pañch Ayat* – a householder who maintains the five sacred fires; five modes of devotion; an almanac, because it enumerates five propitious states; the five products of the cow; a penance of five fires, the fifth being the sun; an epithet of the god of love as he has five arrows; the five digestive fires in the body; the five vestures or wrappers supposed to invest the soul, the earthly body, the vesture of the vital airs, the sensorial and the cognitional, and that of beatitude; the four primary castes of Hindus with the barbarians as fifth; waving five things before an idol and then prostrating oneself before it, a lamp, lotus, cloth, mango and betel leaf; the five life-winds or vital airs. There is a ceremony, *Pañch Bali*, where five kinds of victims are sacrificed, and I have seen hill men conducting this ceremony. A ring or bracelet containing the five metals of gold, silver, bronze, iron and copper, the

Pañch Ratna, is a token of deep respect and significance. Both Hinduism and Buddhism have five great sins but only the former has a Brahman having to perform five daily sacrifices.

Buddhism seems happier than Hinduism with even numbers, despite the Hindu ten-day festival of Dashera. There are four sublime verities and an eightfold way that leads to Nirvana. The Chinese, in particular, seem very intrigued with numbers, especially with the four-character phrases that pepper the conversations of the learnéd, and five-year plans are a common adjunct of central planning. '5 star accompany moon' is a Cantonese dish. The Chinese indefinite number with a connotation of a long time is 100, an example of which is the number of years after which a bamboo grove has to be pruned.

In contrast, the Western world does not like numbers nearly so much, until one comes across service planners who allot numbers to units and formations to a degree that is esoteric if not mystical or even unnecessary. At one time the regular British Army boasted two battalions of the Oxfordshire and Buckinghamshire Light Infantry, despite the main catchment area for the soldiers being London. The Oxfordshire battalion, the 43rd of Foot, waged a bitter war on the Buckinghamshire battalion, the 52nd of Foot. I can remember my father telling me of one of the latter battalion's contempt for the former being shown by his stropping his cut-throat razor every morning fifty-two times, counting out loud until he reached his battalion number. He would count '40, 41, 42', then spit and continue '44, 45'. Any student of military historical minutiae, especially the gunners and their battery numbers, can only express amazement at the time-wasting dedication that goes into the allocation of such details. Where the serviceman's civilian counterpart seems mesmerised, in everyday life, is with 50s, 100s, 1,000s and millions, which have their own magic, be it in relation to anniversaries, cricket scores or the amount of money in the bank. Yet there are old songs with a numbers motive, 'Ten Green Bottles', 'The Twelve Days of Christmas' and that which starts 'This is number one/And the fun has just begun' all spring to mind, as does one that ends up 'And one for the Platoon Commander/Up to his waist in water'.

Nowadays, maybe the numbers to be scored on the football pools keep more people expectant than any others, except for the recruit under the drill sergeant on the square, who knows that his luckiest numbers must, for the immediate future at least, be 1 (pause) 2, 3, 1 (pause) 2, 3, 1 – and end on that self-targeting '1'.

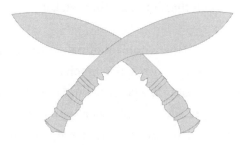

Bangkok Embassy Prowler Guard

The Bangkok Embassy Night Prowler Guard was thought to be idle in doing its duties. In 1974, the ambassador, Mr Arthur de la Mare, a Channel Islander, told me he was anti-Gurkha and needed a good reason to get rid of them as embassy guards. He thought up a scheme whereby he would catch the prowler guard out and so have his good reason to change the guard set-up, thus getting rid of the Gurkhas. So one night around midnight, dressed in slacks and a white shirt, he left the residency by the front door, which he locked behind him. He saw no prowler guard nor could he find one as he went to the main guard at the main gate.

'I had keys for the two wicket gates that led on to a side road,' and made his way to one of them. Still no sign of any prowler guard. 'As I unlocked the gate on my own, I'll get him,' he told me. He relocked the gate, turned too quickly and fell off the small bridge into the dirty, roadside 'khlong'.

Cursing – he had a short fuse – he scrambled out, soaking, smelly and covered in duckweed. He stormed down the road and entered the embassy grounds again through the other wicket gate. Still no signs of any prowler guard.

"'I've got you. I'll sack the whole lot of you," I said to myself,' he told me. He got back to his residence, foul tempered and turned to open the front door. As he did, there was a voice behind him: "Anything else sir?"

'I turned and there was the prowler sentry, soaked, smelly and covered in duckweed. I was shaken rigid and after that I trusted the Gurkhas so I kept them on as embassy guards,' he said.

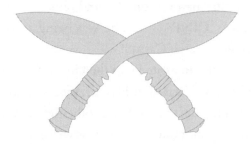

A Beached Submariner

1970: I was commandant of the Jungle Warfare School in Kota Tinggi, Johore, in Peninsular Malaysia, which was responsible for running courses in counter-revolutionary (Chinese-inspired communist revolution) warfare. To teach students about the threat of an Asian enemy they had to know more than a plain 'military' dimension on the subject, which was, basically, how to fight, move and live in the jungle. They had to understand their Asian enemy. For the record, between 1964 and 1970 around 900 military men came to be trained a year and more than a quarter of them came from the Army of the Republic of Vietnam (ARVN); half were British forces, including Gurkhas, the remainder were from North and South America, Africa, Australasia and thirteen 'free world' Asian countries.

One day in 1970 we had an unusually important visitor. This in itself was nothing out of the ordinary and operating as we did, like the rest of the British Army, on a shoestring as far as staff went (which was not very far) I had to lead most of them myself. I had to 'field' eight visitors every five working days for more than three years, so many that I can now only recall the most unusual of them. They were military men, journalists, television teams, scientists, politicians, financiers, of every stripe. However, this man was one I could remember as his pedigree announced him as 'CINPAC' and he was being accompanied by a 'POLAD'! Shades of Lewis Carroll!

I discovered that this translated into the United States' Commander-in-Chief Pacific Forces, based in Hawaii, who was so powerful that Vietnam was merely a fief to a flank. The other set of initials showed he was accompanied by his political adviser, as well as a personal assistant and a personal physician. Other details showed me that he had served as a submariner.

The great day saw the great man and his team arrive. After briefing them I took them to where a Jungle Wing Course was being lectured. It was a large hall, with seats rising in serried rows. CINCPAC, I cannot recall his name, was built as I am, not more than 5½ft tall, lithe and spare. I took him to the front of the assembled group, turned and faced the students.

I told them who was with me and proceeded to tell CINCPAC who was who. Mystery showed itself on his weather-beaten face – not battle-scarred, nor even 'bottle-scarred' as a pre-war Penang newspaper described a new governor's face in succeeding editions. The course commander was from the British office of Gurkhas; the lecturer was an Australian gunnery officer. Students were from all five continents: South America – Guyana; Africa – Ghana; Asia – Thais, Singaporeans, Filipinos and Brunei Malays as well as stalwarts from the Gurkha Contingent of the Singapore Police; the Antipodes had sent Australians and New Zealanders; while, from Britain there were not only army men but men from the Royal Air Force Regiment and the Royal Marines.

A stunned silence followed. CINCPAC gulped, turned to me and in a very audible undertone asked – was it with dismay, disgust or disbelief? – 'And you have no submariners here?'

I turned and, so that all present could hear, said, in the greatest confidence and labouring my syllables, 'Admiral, the greatest submariner in the United States Navy is standing right here beside me.'

A pause, then, in a husky voice, 'God damn it, son. You win!'

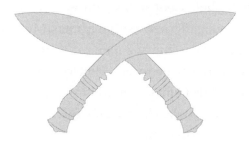

My Long Quest for Survival

'If you hit your head you'll be blind for life.'

By then I had been losing my sight for two years because of cataracts in both eyes. At 57 I was not really old enough to suffer from them and my nagging thought was that, having made 1kg of food last for six and a half days then fifty-two days (and later just a little more for a further seventy then eighty days) when working with the aborigines south of the Thai border in 1961 and 1962, my 'hunger-strike' scale of rations were having their dreaded effect at last – although the Veterans Department later said that nothing I had done during my service was responsible for such a condition so there was no case for a medical pension.

When deputy recruiting officer in west Nepal, so painful was normal light that I had to walk under an umbrella on trek and Buddhiman, my surrogate son, had to lead me. British Medical Hopsital (BMH) Dharan received my call forward instructions from BMH in Hong Kong but did not tell me about it for six months. When I did go, I had to be escorted on to the plane in Kathmandu: Bangkok, where I changed planes, was radioed to help me. There my luggage was mislaid and only when it was found did I go through customs when no planeload of people was present so the inspector was suspicious. I could not see

191

his face or the keyhole to open my suitcase but felt my key into it. Luckily I knew enough Thai to explain matters. My connecting flight was delayed by six hours and at 3 a.m. the next morning I told the Hong Kong taxi driver to go to the 'Military Hospital' in Cantonese but the 'military' eluded him so I nearly went to the civilian hospital by mistake. I was curtly asked by the duty sister why I was late: 'Sister, ask the pilot,' was my rejoinder.

I was put in the matron's emergency room at the back of the pregnant women's ward – 'quiet' – and, after the first eye was operated on I did not realise I was no longer in my old room. I stumbled to where I thought the lavatory was and, only just in time, was stopped from pissing on the pregnant women's TV set. Once back in bed an excited nurse came and said, 'Wobble your toes, wobble your toes.' I weakly muttered, 'Sister, it's my eyes not my toes,' but wobble my toes I did. I had been given too much 'knock out' dope and thrombosis was feared.

'If you hit your head you'll be blind for life,' said the eye specialist, looking grim that day I was discharged in far-off June 1981 when both lens had been successfully removed by cutting each eye open, lifting off the lens, then stitching both up again. Six months later I went back to have the knots of the stitches removed.

The thought of blindness has ever haunted me, especially in the six months it took to learn how to walk with tunnel vision specs, half the power of binoculars, and hanging on to Buddhiman lest I fell. The intimacy was total: I still trekked (more than 1,000 miles a year), he helping me strip and bathe in the rivers, taking me out in the evening before bed, righting me when I overbalanced and stopping other walkers from bumping into me. I then knew that, after I left the army, he was the only one on whom I could depend totally. I had left England on 8 June 1944 and, except for far fewer leaves than entitled, I had not properly lived in England post-war – after so much time and as a single man I had no one to go back to. The gulf between my wish for Buddhiman to look after me and governmental rules prohibiting him from doing so seemed unbridgeable.

Yet Dame Fortune managed a smile: as I left Nepal at the end of my service in 1982 I was asked to join the university's Research Centre for Nepal and Asian studies in Kirtipur as an assistant reader. I accepted with gratitude and joined six months later. At a symposium for 'higher Nepalese learning' the youngest royal prince was the chief guest and the vice chancellor pulled me out to be presented. 'Why do you want to stay here in Nepal?' he asked. 'Because I want to repay all that I have learnt of how to bear hardship and fortitude from your subjects, Sarkar, by some personal contribution,' thinking both of ten years spent in the jungle and my eyes.

In 1985 the outgoing ambassador, the late John Denson, asked the protocol officer how I could approach the king about permanency in Nepal. The result, after ten nail-biting months, was being given permanent residential status with the unique privilege of being the only foreigner ever in the history of the country to be a house and land owner. That granted, I started life with Buddhiman, Bhimkumari and a growing family, in Pokhara.

How to stay permanently in Nepal still worried me – before requesting citizenship a preliminary fifteen-year stay with a non-tourist visa (but not for any foreign organisation) was mandatory. I got mine because I had been in the university.

After twenty years I was blithely told that the probationary time was only twenty years. There were four aspects to be covered and I had only completed the one of sufficient time in incubation. The other three were giving up the passport of the land of one's birth, a good knowledge of spoken and written Nepali, and making sufficient contributions for 'general welfare', plus always having a minimum of $20,000 in the bank.

In 2002 I renounced my British citizenship by giving in my passport and paying £20 for the privilege before asking for Nepalese citizenship. The process is Byzantine and awe-inspiring in its complexity, frustrating in its obscurity and time-consuming in its progress from ward to sub-metropolis to district to ward to sub-metropolis to district to district police to ward police to a 'five good men and true' jury sitting with me and a sub-inspector to pronounce on whether I was a fit subject for being awarded citizenship – each signing twice on two handwritten copies of what the policeman had noted – to ward police to district police to district.

Matters came to a halt as the proper form for the obligatory covering letter forwarding the paperwork to the ministry was not in stock nor were there any forms in the ministry itself. Eventually the 'special covering letter' was allowed to be handwritten. Twice I had to have my thumb prints on the page, with the left thumb on the right of the pair and the right thumb on the left. On the eve of the very last signature of approval all local government officials were dismissed in a political shake-up. Against all odds I did get 'that' signature but, even so, the whole lot was again nearly scuppered because the ink was blue, not red. Now a six-month wait for an answer, thought I in my total ignorance.

Later on that year I was invited to the opening ceremony of a seven-day religious marathon, in a village where I had materially helped its school, to raise funds to establish a 'campus' in the existing school complex. There a senior and well-known pundit told me he was the chairman of the World Hindu Council and had heard I had been a help to various people and places, so he was inviting me to become an honorary member of his organisation. He would give me a certificate to that effect and tell the king, with whom he was in regular contact. To be a Hindu one must be born Hindu and there is neither method nor ceremony for conversion as it is technically impossible to convert to Hinduism, it being as much a social system as a religion.

So, after deep consideration, I found I was not unsympathetic to the idea as by then I regarded all 'historical' religions and their many divine and religious 'personalities' – whose original had a larger than normal essence of the 'divine spark', with many as allegoric icons and the name of the religion being irrelevant provided that the correct 'path' was recognised as such – and I wished to embrace wisdom wherever I could find it. Nor do I believe that a showing of the 'divine spark' is necessarily exclusive to one individual once a millennium. For me it boils down to a leaning towards a 'literalist' approach of holy scriptures and beliefs, which I have eschewed more and more over the years, or towards a gnostic bias with a Deist approach. My Christianity is, therefore, 'ethical' in content as I have nothing better, nor will I. Added to that, Buddhiman assured me that being an honorary Hindu did not mean I had to accept the Hindu 'panoply' literally or claim that faith as my own. Having already been elected an honorary life member of the local, and biggest, Buddhist Crematorium Committee, I could only recall what my grandmother had taught me when I was a small boy: 'Said the bishop when asked to a feast – where he ate almost nothing but yeast – I may not rise as high as my God in the sky, but I want to get started, at least.'

In 2003 the pundit told me that when he last went to put a *tika* on the king's forehead he mentioned that I had not heard the outcome of my quest for Nepalese citizenship. By then I was even more fully aware that every day with sight was a bonus. I knew of nowhere else I could be looked after with so much love and happiness, so my Pokhara home had to be my 'last nest'.

(I had recently heard about an Englishman who had applied for Turkish citizenship, the only such case ever apparently. He had to be certified as sane before being recommended as suitable for such a status and that meant visiting a Turkish psychiatrist who could find nothing wrong with him. 'You are perfectly sane: why did you come to me?' he asked. 'I want to become a Turkish citizen,' the Englishman explained. 'Then you must be mad,' countered the psychiatrist but I do not know if that officially barred the Englishman from becoming Turkish or not.)

In 2004 I was made an official adviser for the royal visit to Pokhara in April–May. I had been told I would be granted an audience so I could ask the king about my citizenship as by then I had had no answer in twenty-two months. But the royal programme was curtailed by two weeks so there were no audiences for any of the 137 people who had put their names down for one. Apparently the king told one local official who did manage an audience and who asked about me that he thought that he had already authorised it for me. My inability to get a decision and the sadness in the country generally was always with me, like an elusive shadow hovering on the very edge of my field of vision, sensed but never seen.

That same year in one week one English-language and three Nepali-language newspapers published articles about my lack of citizenship. According to the palace, the home minister and the ambassador, no new citizenship papers were to be given to anyone until some new law was enacted – there was no likelihood of such a law as long as the country was in Maoist turmoil.

In 2005 King Gyanendra visited Pokhara and I put in an official application for my quest to be looked into. When he took a walk along the road Buddhiman gave him another copy with a photo of the family inside the envelope. Also I had a long talk with the Lord Lieutenant (LL) prior to the royal visit and gave him a copy of the official paperwork as well as an application to be considered an honorary citizen – 'belt and braces'. The king had a private meal with the LL and ordered photostat copies of all the paperwork, which he put into his inside coat pocket.

Yet nothing happened.

On 26 March 2006 the largest and oldest high school in Pokhara held its golden jubilee. The king and queen were chief guests. I, who had helped it and its Blind Section financially, was invited and given the privilege of being in the receiving line to welcome their majesties. Each had to be given a bouquet of flowers as well as a *namaste* in the act of presenting them. I was told to speak in Nepali. I said, 'Your Majesty, I have been with Nepalis for sixty-one years, three months and sixteen days. I have completely given up everything in England and my humble prayer is for citizenship and that you will order it.' He nodded and mumbled a yes as I gave him his flowers but passed on too quickly for me to give him the paperwork still in my inner coat pocket. I had to be ready for the queen, who followed in quick succession, to receive her bouquet. I managed to get my petition delivered through the Lord Lieutenant but, in spite of my written request being the fifth that had found its way into the palace office, I got no answer.

I was sometimes asked if the frustration did not send me ballistic and give me duodenal ulcers? My answer was that when there was any problem that would infuriate a Westerner I looked on it as a Nepali would, and was unconcerned; and were a Nepali to become ballistic I looked on it as a Westerner would so it left me unruffled. Then a new lot in the government came up with the suggestion that no foreigner be allowed to have Nepalese citizenship. Nobody acted on the suggestion because, in fact, that was already the case.

Later that same year, keeping in touch with local officialdom, I showed my paperwork to the senior functionary in the district office. He read it thoroughly, then accused me of breaking the law of the land. I asked him how so? I was accused of not having had a visa stamped in my passport for five years, a grave transgression. I explained that the very process of citizenship could not start until the original passport has been surrendered, with a certificate from the original country's Home Office to that effect. I was ordered to get my passport back, have it stamped five times and return it – in other words, wholly negating the original process by making me start afresh. He would not have it otherwise. I left the office, speechless – a most rare occurrence for me.

The world is divided into two types of people: those who say 'What to do?' and those who ask 'How to do it?' I wrote a letter to the UK Home Office asking them to let the Nepalese equivalent understand that I did not accept that dilatoriness of the Nepalese government in answering my request was reason enough for cancelling my original renunciation and asking for my passport back before cancelling it for a second time (only very seldom, if ever, allowed). I sent the letter by registered Nepalese mail and had several photocopies of my original letter made with a photo of the post office receipt on the top of the page. Never did answer ensue: I also sent a copy to the British consul here in Nepal – no response from there either.

Later still, Buddhiman and a minister, whom thirty years earlier as a schoolboy I had made laugh, went and saw the functionary who would put the 'chop' on my citizenship papers. Positive. Hooray! Buddhiman and a lawyer fixed with said functionary, by phone, to meet on a certain day, which happened to be the day the Maoists left the government and Kathmandu erupted. Cancel mission. As one might say, every silver lining has its cloud. Trying to get any governmental decision in Nepal is as hard as trying to put one's thumb on a blob of quicksilver.

My detractors will say that I had 'gone native', was 'hill top' and 'rice minded' and that I had 'broken the mould'; those who understand will see it as my quest for survival as I was slipping slowly and relentlessly into blindness.

In 2008 a TV reporter went to see the chief district officer (CDO) and, off his own bat, asked him why there had been such inactivity around my application. His answer was that the case was being looked into. The next day the reporter came round and I gave him a half-hour-plus interview. I am always careful in what I say under such circumstances: to try to be clever is unwise. A week later I learnt that the reporter had once more gone to the CDO's office and, quite how I know not, got him to ring the relevant section in the home ministry and demand a positive result.

Yet nothing happened until 2009 when we were rung up at 10 p.m. one Friday and told to be at the ruling party's senior member's house at 9 a.m. on the following Sunday to be 'vetted' and, if successful, the home minister would be ordered to let me talk to him about my seven-year wait. The senior member asked me why I had not got citizenship to which my answer was 'don't ask me why I have not got it, ask those who should give it to me why they haven't'. I met the home minister and found that we both worked in the same research centre twenty-five years before. He told me I would hear positively within four to six weeks. I never did.

How such a call came is complicated but, in brief, Buddhiman's cousin, A, had a schoolboy friend, B. I had given a talk to his school about eighteen years before, which he remembered. B was by then a police inspector in the ministry building. B's friend, C, also a police inspector, had a friend, D, a pleader living in the east of the country, who is a nephew of E, a one-time assistant prime minister. D came to Kathmandu, knowing about me, and told his uncle E, that I was in my 85th year and needed looking after. E, knowing that F, the home minister, would be out of the country some time in the near future, called us at his 'earliest'. I told F that I wanted him to chase up my file that my eyes had taken a turn for the worse in the past month (I couldn't recognise people from ten paces away and could only read with difficulty) so to let me have Nepal as my last refuge.

Slow forward to 2011: I had now waited for more than nine years for an answer to my request. I wrote a letter to the prime minister, which was given him when he visited Pokhara and I was at the same function; I wrote a similar letter to the deputy prime minister, he who two years earlier had called me to Kathmandu. The leader of the Young Communist League reported my case to the senior Maoist leader, who said he would take up my case. I hoped that whatever I wrote in my letters wouldn't get me accused of committing a malfeasance by sophistry or casuistry. I had recently learnt that Human Rights, Nepal, had, off its own bat, taken my case up. It was sobering that ex-Gurkha officers of my old Indian Army battalion, 1/1 GR, had also twice been to the Home Ministry on my behalf but no such efforts had been made by similar ex-members of the Brigade of Gurkhas.

Mother of ironies, the younger brother of the founder of the Communist Party of Nepal asked me why I was not a citizen. My answer, in my dotage, could be based on the Gospel according to St Matthew: 22: 21, where, instead of rendering to Caesar Caesar's and to God God's, put bumbledom vs common sense – but keeping very quiet about it. I have none of the three most precious currencies of all politicians: position, preferment and patronage. Instead, living as I do, I only see the underside of the tapestry of Nepalese life. What I had already done was to write a letter to a future British ambassador in Kathmandu that Buddhiman would take to the embassy if I died before getting citizenship and in which I asked the ambassador to 'take my case' to the head of state and say such treatment was not the way to keep good relations between Britain and Nepal.

On 6 December 2011, the president of Federal and Democratic Nepal visited Pokhara to open a campus that had been operative for twenty-five years already. The committee arranging events put me on it with a view to telling the president that it was about time I had Nepalese citizenship, having waited more than nine years for an answer. The day before the opening, two campus stalwarts visited the president and told him, in great detail, about me. Before he arrived at the campus, the master of ceremonies mentioned my name to the assembled hundreds and asked the reporters to publish my case. In my letter to the president I also copied the letters I had written to the past two prime ministers, a deputy prime minister and the home minister. To go any higher would have to be to the stratospheric supranational! As the president swept out of the hall accompanied by so many people jostling him – my mind irreverently comparing it to a pack of dogs after a bitch on heat – I was pulled off my chair, Buddhiman leading me. The president he stopped in front of me. 'Please accept these flowers,' I said, giving him a bunch, 'and this, my humble request,' and put the envelope in his hands. I then gave him a short Nepali proverb – invoking the goddess of success, one might say – and he took it, smiling. But this also resulted in nothing: four months later I learnt that the president had given my paperwork to his office secretary, who refused to touch it. I have to admit I felt deflated and asked myself what can one expect from any government that makes its decisions viscerally and not cerebrally?

In 2012 on a morning walk I passed the Armed Forces Police (AFP) Training College and found out that the next passing out parade was to be on the following Friday and that the chief guest was the newish Maoist prime minister. Buddhiman and I, dressed smartly, went to see the AFP commandant to ask him for an invitation. After the parade we were called into the presence. I apologised for taking up his time and told him that we had not met for twenty-eight years. Sitting next to him out came my story with a large retinue listening in with 'pin-drop' silence. I got them all laughing. 'I'll get it fixed, don't worry,' said the PM. No need to say that nothing eventuated.

In 2013 I had an unexpected visit from a freelance Nepalese journalist about my lack of citizenship: the result? Nothing in Nepal but headlines in Hong Kong's *South China Morning Post*. Soon after that, talking to one of the Maoist foot soldiers now wearing plain clothes, the subject of my (lack of) citizenship came up. Saddened, he personally went to the ministry to help me: on hearing the word 'colonel' the functionary rubbed finger and thumb together, despite the ex-foot soldier telling him how much I had already offered the country.

Being a permanent resident I was lucky in that I did have crumpled leaves, not thorns, to lie on. Over the long years without the safety of citizenship, to keep safe I have had to show zeal without fire and intelligence without talent, never to cause an argument nor display any unredeeming vices: 'when the pen writes a poem it need not understand the verse and whether the pot be whole or broken, it still stands witness to the work of the potter.'

And so at last to 2014: towards the end of August the British ambassador, his first secretary and defence attaché had an audience with the president of Nepal and handed over an official government of Great Britain letter asking that J.P. Cross, now in his 90th year, be granted Nepalese citizenship 'in the spirit of G200' – I was only told about it after it had happened and I was in no way responsible for it. It was entirely at the initiative of the defence attaché, Colonel Sean Harris. I had thought that, having tried not to be British, the British ambassador would have nothing to do with me. But I was wrong. Colonel Harris read out a report of what I had done for the country and its individuals, including the way I had managed to help alleviate famine, in 1978, by reporting on conditions to the British ambassador, who asked London for help. When the answer came back in the negative saying that the only help being offered was two RAF Hercules aircraft and 20,000 tons of rice to Cambodia, the ambassador replied that if Lieutenant Colonel J.P. Cross recommended help how could it be refused? My name, being known, 'worked the oracle' and help was split half and half between Cambodia and Nepal. Colonel Harris told me that I was then on the cusp of getting Nepalese citizenship.

A few weeks later, Buddhiman and I drove into the ministerial complex, an unbelievably difficult feat for a non-ministerial person. This was the result of my having sown a seed all of thirty-eight years earlier. In brief, the primary school in Buddhiman's village needed money. From my 'aid' budget I could afford 1 *lakh* rupees (100,000) but the Nepalese government allowed nothing above 10,000. I got over that problem by telling the authorities that nine villagers had given me an IOU for 10,000 rupees each so the *lakh* was accounted for. The headmaster of that time never forgot that and, by 2014, was a *sachib*, secretary, in the Statistics Branch of the Home Ministry so, with him, we were able to let us drive into the ministry without any trouble. There the citizenship *sachib* told me that there should be no trouble in getting citizenship from now onward but … the 'jury' papers (known as *muchulka*) were missing from my file and without them nothing could move forward. We were told to get the office copy from the Pokhara CDO's office but after a four-day search nothing came to light so we started all over again. This took two sessions, one of four hours' duration and the other of six. The police had to check me – was I suffering from any disease, was I a drunkard or a fornicator, was I a breaker of laws (the only law I have broken is the law of averages), was I involved in politics, what did I do in my spare time and other intrusive questions. Buddhiman answered them: no health problems but a man in his 90th year has bad eyes and ears.

The new papers went to the ministry and shortly afterwards, on 13 November, we had a phone call, 'Come to the ministry tomorrow.' This we did, again only with the help of the ex-head, and at 1 p.m. on 14 November 2014 I became the second-ever Brit to become a Nepalese citizen, after a wait of thirty-two years, the equivalent time a new recruit takes to earn his Gurkha major's pension. The first award of citizenship, fifty years ago, was to the lady who started the Pokhara leprosarium. There are 200 foreign aspirants waiting for their citizenship. And the missing *muchulka* was seen in the file, 'misplaced', while some junior clerk had put all my written requests over the years in a file that lay unopened until after my first visit to the ministry – a turpitudinous peccadillo?

On our return my family was ecstatically vivacious: hugs, garlands, bunches of flowers, a cake with 'firework' candles, the lot. I was most touched on my first morning walk when, called over by the driver of a water tanker, I was told that the previous driver had contacted him to congratulate me – from California! I have been deeply, deeply humbled at the great joy shown by so many Nepalis in the country and from every continent except Latin America: beyond expectation and even imagination.

One national Nepali-language newspaper published my story on the morrow, with my photo, on the front page; another had most of the front-page story plus photo; the leading national English-language paper had my photo; while the local Pokhara newspaper also carried the story and the local FM radio broadcast it. Talk about 'knocking a nail out of sight'.

If and when the worst happens to my eyes, my long struggle for survival being finally over, I will now be safe with my wonderful Nepalese family: 'going native', then 'becoming native', was a price well worth paying in full, whatever others may say behind my back.

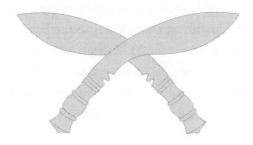

'J.P. Cross has Gone Native' – Correct or Not?

At the tender age of 19 I left England on 8 June 1944 for India and joined a Gurkha regiment on 10 December on commissioning that same year. Since then I have spent the whole of my adult life in Asia, with Gurkhas in the army until 1982 and living in Nepal ever since.

Soon after leaving the army I visited England. A reporter from the local *Bournemouth Gazette* asked me about my relationship with the Gurkhas, to which my answer was, 'Do I love because I understand or do I understand because I love?'

That was too deep for him to publish and probably as deep as I will ever get. My answer, some thirty years later is still, 'Not sure but does it matter?' But whichever way any emphasis is laid, one aspect is certain: Gurkhas in particular and Nepalis in general have responded in just proportion, both by what they have said and by how they have said it; in other words, by their reaction to me, by hint, inference or gesture.

This caused many brother officers, chiefly behind my back, to say, 'Oh! J.P. Cross has gone native!' 'Why?' I have asked myself. 'Provided military discipline was maintained, such a bond of empathy stimulated an increase in efficiency and, at times, medical recovery that could not otherwise have been engendered.' And military discipline was maintained, even though my soldiers smiled more often at me than at others. 'With you we know no fear,' was said more than once, as was, 'You see into our guts and we cannot tell you a lie.'

Five of many examples of when I was told by that 'only you, *Saheb*, could have done it' are, briefly:

- operating, on the Malay–Thai border, on 1kg of food for six and half days then fifty-two days, carrying weights more than bodyweight for six days, then for seventy days, and five and half days, then for eighty, with no grumbling and no sickness. (This was because we were operationally not allowed any resupply so had to carry all our food; I had asked the medical officer the least each day to prevent starvation: '5oz', so I 'upped' that to 5½. I have fully described the operations in my quaintly named *A Face Like A Chicken's Backside*;

- dropping, for the first time ever in the British Army in south-east Asia, two plane loads of 'simultaneous 20s', without one man having to be checked in pre- or in-flight checks – the RAF Parachute School staff told me that they would not have believed such was possible if they had not seen it themselves;

- influencing a dying man who would not eat to eat. He eventually did and lived;

- giving so much of myself (*pneuma*? spirit?) to a cataleptic murderer that he, after total silence for months, explained why he had murdered and when I felt I could no longer sustain myself I pulled myself back inside me – the murderer slumped and never spoke again;

- giving of myself, weekly for a month, to a leper, who had taken no solid food for a year. The doctor in charge of the leprosarium called his recovery 'miraculous'.

Dreams also tell their own story of mental linkage: three times when on trek in the mountains from my unit has my presence been known about only from dreams, once in a six-month bracket of my arrival in a man's house (so he had prepared a party for me) and twice with no previous knowledge a man came to meet me not having met me for five years and another not having met me for ten, both times when as serving soldiers.

Language may also play a part: although I did not start learning Nepali until I was just short of 20 years old, no Nepali takes me for a foreigner on hearing me speak. Likewise religion: I have been invited to become an honorary Hindu and an honorary Buddhist – and accepted both. But, even before that, there was 'something other' that people wanted from me: occasionally first-time pregnant mothers want blessings so that their first born be a son; lads to be successful recruits for the British Army; and countless students for passing exams. My success rate is astonishingly high!

The cause of such empathy was intriguingly stimulated when, living in Nepal after I had left the army, I was visited by an English woman who looked after ill Gurkha soldiers in Aldershot. She had read a book I had written. 'I presumed you were just another stuffy old colonel when I saw the title but having read it I knew I was wrong,' she told me, adding how she had known that, in a previous existence as a Nepali, she had been sick and left to die in Kathmandu. In the 1950s, visiting Kathmandu, two eminent men had come to her hotel to ask her if she would stay on and nurse the sick. 'I told them I only nursed the young and in England.' Her negative reaction shocked the hotel manager, who obviously had great respect for the visitors, who accepted her refusal and politely left. They were the crown prince and an aide.

She, half jokingly I hoped, said that probably she and I had been married Nepalis in some previous incarnation. I told her that many Nepalis thought that I had once been born a Nepali and that there was one man, Mandhoj Dura, in our hill village whose lifelong prophesies, however outlandish, had never been wrong. He had, in a trance, said that my surrogate son, Buddhiman, and I had been born of the same mother in a Christian country to the east, so I told her. The nearest 'Christian country to the east' could best refer to the one-time Malla kingdom in the Kathmandu valley when, for maybe a century and a half, Capuchin priests had lived and practised there. They were expelled only in 1768. We would be together again in the future. (By then King Birendra had given me the accolade of being the only foreigner, including Indians, to be a house and land owner in my own name.)

So Buddhiman and I went back to ask Mandhoj three questions about our past, our future and who had been my wife? The first two questions were answered as before, after much laboriously shaking intercourse with the gods that Mandhoj, now deep in a trance, was addressing but, so tired was he by then that the wife question was never answered.

Ever since the strange occurrences of his youth, when, at the age of 9, he was taken by a spirit of the forest for two days and taught a number of special skills, such as reading the future and communicating with either the dead or the unborn, Mandhoj had had the power of prophecy. It was proved time and time again. He became a soldier in the Assam Regiment and married Buddhiman's aunt on his first leave. Back in his unit, his foot stuck in a stirrup as he was getting off a horse and it ran away, dragging him for quite a long way, severely bumping his head. He became completely deaf. He must have broken both eardrums. He was lucky not to lose his life.

Just one more example of his extraordinary power: Buddhiman's younger brother's future father-in-law, Singabahadur, was told by Mandhoj that it was better not to enlist in the Gurkha Contingent of the Singapore Police. Enlist he did and the nearer he got to Singapore the mistier it became, so was soon returned to an unmisty Nepal. Singabahadur then asked Mandhoj what would happen if he joined the Indian Army. Pension difficulties, was the answer, otherwise no problem. Thirty-two years later, Honorary Captain Singabahadur Gurung was only allowed the pension of an honorary lieutenant.

And our possible pre-existence was told us by one Tekbahadur Chhetri, a civilian. In 2014, aged about 50, he met us, knowing nothing whatsoever about us. But he had had an unusual youth, on several occasions finding himself walking alone, not consciously knowing where he was or how he'd got there. One night, when 9 years of age, something like lightning flashed and he was picked up and taken to a pond in a field. He was stood up, feet in mud-like quicksand with only his head showing. Only on the third day was he rescued. The clothes he had been wearing were not found.

But, as he recovered, he found he could see the souls of the dead, especially those of infants whose unwanted bodies had been drowned. He trembled at the start of the two weeks of bright moon and again at the start of the two dark weeks. By then he could read the past and the future but only after he had placed, in a small mound, exactly 1lb of unhusked rice on a plate and, for several minutes, stroking it with the second and third fingers of his right hand, muttering while he did.

He knew nothing about either of us, had never heard about us nor had he ever seen us. This is what he had to say to us, having stroked the rice we had got for him:

- both Buddhiman and I had been together in a previous life but had become separated;
- Buddhiman's father had died of lockjaw when he ran a piece of wood into his foot when ploughing. True;
- Buddhiman never swore at anyone. True;
- gave blessings to people. He does;
- does not eat certain types of meat. True;
- will look after me as I have given him everything, even my soul and I can't manage without him. (With my poor eyes, exactly so.)

As for me:

- I would eventually become a citizen of Nepal (by then the unfinished process had taken over thirty years).
- I had given all my money to my Nepalese family and had none myself. True;

- I was unmarried. My first attempt when young should have been successful so all the other attempts were bound to be unsuccessful;
- I had no sins in me and did what I said I'd do;
- I would be reincarnated. If good, as a man; if not, as a bird. (Is this why I can imitate a cuckoo, a dove, a cock and a turkey, to say nothing of whistling like the Malayan great eared nightjar so well they answer me?)

So, readers all, take a deep breath before I am laughed out of court – not for the first time either – that some part of my former Nepalese dæmon was reborn in my present incarnation of Christian, English parents, so making me a twin of sorts with myself. In other words, the verb 'gone' is incorrect because my original Nepalese dæmon has continued to influence my present life in a way the vast majority of all people never experience.

So what should the verb be? I like to think of it as 'is', native English in England and native Nepali in Nepal. Also, as an afterthought, that is most likely the reason why I have seemed unconventional at times.

I rest my case, M'Lud, whether you agree with me or not. As a nonagenarian, I don't mind either way.

1/1 Gorkha Rifles: 200th Anniversary

24 April 2015

I had to laugh; I just couldn't help it on that morning of 20 April 2015 when I walked across the Nepalese border into India. Oh mother of delicious ironies! I'll come to that in a moment, however. First of all I must tell you that I joined the 1st King George V's Own Gurkha Rifles (Malaun Regiment) when I was commissioned on 10 December 1944. I served in the first battalion for the last few months of the Burma war and left it on 23 November 1947 when I was wrongly sent to the 2nd Gurkhas in Dehradun before being correctly posted to 1/7 Gurkha Rifles in Rangoon, Burma.

I live in Pokhara, Nepal, and had been told I would be invited to the battalion's 200th anniversary celebrations about three years earlier and was determined not to miss my last chance to visit it. I had been back twice before, once in old 1st Gurkha Rifles, Regimental Centre cantonment at Dharmsala in 1959 and again for the 175th anniversary celebrations, held in Poona, now Puné, in 1990. Both times I naturally travelled on my British passport but now the question of travel documents, or rather the lack of them, haunted me. In 1976 I had been posted to west Nepal as a recruiter. In 1981 both my eyes had the lens extracted and I was told I'd be permanently blinded if I hit my head. Immediately after retiring on pension in 1982 I'd been asked to serve as a researcher in the Tribhuvan University in Kathmandu. I had not had a home posting since leaving England on 8 June 1944; thirty-eight years previously so my surrogate son, Buddhiman Gurung, and his wife, became my lodestones for survival if I were to become blind, meaning I had to continue to live in Nepal. In 1984 King Birendra had given me permanent residential status with the privilege of being a house and land owner – the only foreigner in the history of the country ever to be so honoured. But the political situation became dire after the overthrow of the monarchy in 2008, with many previous royal symbols becoming anathema to the 'new-look' governments. Would my unique status be revoked? If so, what to do? I felt mentally cowed.

The answer, for permanence and peace of mind, was to apply for Nepalese citizenship. Easier said than done – getting it that is, not the actual applying, which is relatively simple although the ensuing ramifications were labyrinthine. Without renouncing citizenship of the land of one's birth – meaning giving up my passport and getting a certificate to that effect from the Foreign and Commonwealth Office – the actual processing does not start even after a prescribed wait of, in my case, twenty years. I had thought I'd have an answer after six months but after ten years of hearing nothing positive, despite many requests, I began to fret as 2015 loomed nearer and nearer. I had no citizenship, so no passport; no passport, no visa; no visa, no visit to India so no anniversary celebrations.

Then the Gurkha network came into play: the first CO of Buddhiman's wife's third brother's battalion, 2/8 GR, became the Indian Army's Defence attaché in Kathmandu. That somehow meant it was easier to make contact with him than otherwise. He told me to write to the Indian ambassador, explaining the situation and asking for a visa with no passport a year and a half before 'the day' – so long ahead because 'one cannot hurry the East'. In my letter I said that I still got 1/1 GR party invitations, Part I Orders and Dashera presents. I asked for a month's visa and was surprised when told that this would be stamped on my invitation paperwork. Who said that governments can't be flexible if approached correctly?

On 14 November 2014, five months before the 200th anniversary celebrations, I was given my Nepalese citizenship, the second Briton ever. But even with an official certificate in my possession, so rare is a European Nepali that, when about to emplane in Kathmandu for an internal flight, a senior policeman drove up and demanded to see it. He took the details, presumably to check with the Home Ministry. I told him when I was given it and he said, with a smile, 'Oh yes', he had read about it in the newspapers and congratulated me. I can only presume that the functionaries at the airport ticket counter had thought I was bogus and reported it to the security authorities!

Buddhiman and I each received our invitation in a large folder. On the cover were the 200th anniversary logo, all six badges the regiment had had since 1815, along with a copy of the GOC-in-C, Northern Command Unit Appreciation of IMDAD, 2005 (a major rescue operation) and inside a brief history and instructions on how to reach the battalion by rail from all over India. On page 3 was the detailed programme and, on the back, a list of honours and awards in two lists: pre-independence with pictures of the Victoria and Military Crosses and post-independence with pictures of the top three current awards.

Early on the morning of the 20th, with more than eighty retired 1/1 GR junior commissioned officers (JCO), some wives and children, having left Pokhara in three buses the day before, we crossed the Nepal–India border, trundling our luggage. I wondered if I'd still be an object of suspicion, but I walked over without either customs or immigration of either country taking the slightest notice of me; that is why I burst out laughing. Although I would never have dared to, I could have walked over without documents and undiscovered!

The battalion was in Pathankot, a twenty-three-hour train ride from our nearest Indian railway station at Gorakhpore. Pre-planning for the anniversary celebrations was time consuming and meticulous: many months prior a team of serving officers had toured Nepal, noting who and from what village wanted to attend. Two servicemen, a junior commissioned officer (JCO) and a havildar accompanied us all the way, there and back, checking bus and train reservations and ensuring that the women and children were properly cared for.

At our destination in the afternoon of the third day, we were met by a major and a *naik* liaison officer (LO), the latter our own, and taken outside where we were given a seat – the last thing I wanted! – and a glass of cold water, proffered to us on a silver salver by a smiling rifleman. Our LO took us to a vehicle, which had my name pasted on the windscreen, with an Indian lance *naik*, not a Gurkha, driver. The journey to Manun Cantonment, the home of 39 Division and 1/1 GR's 90 Brigade, did not take long. Accommodation was tight, with so many (many) guests: Buddhiman and I were billeted in a guest suite of the Sovereign Sixteenth, 16 Dogra Regiment, with our own Gurkha batman. A handwritten welcome from the CO and his wife awaited us.

Our first event was dinner on the morrow with the commanding officer, from 8 p.m. until after midnight. Among the guests were previous colonels of the regiment, commanding officers as well as local dignitaries. As the only pre-independence British officer there, many spoke to me although I actually knew only a few folk, such as a doctor who had served in the Indian Embassy pension paying office – pension camp, in short – in Pokhara and the CO from the 175th anniversary.

The next morning the programme started in earnest. As we drove to the temple for a dedication, I noticed how spruce and tidy the battalion lines were; how battle honours written on milestones on either side of the road leading to battalion HQ 'brought history home'; how smart the sentries were on the road, wearing a regimental choker and calling our their salaams as we passed. At the temple were two pandits, the elder I knew from before and whose brother-in-law's father had taught me the Devanagri script in 1946. The service was graced by the colonel of the regiment, Lieutenant General Ravi Thodge, the master general of ordnance, who had been in charge of the Indian pension camp and a friend twenty-eight years earlier.

We moved off to an 'interaction' where a weapons and equipment display was laid out, with, nearby, a scaled model of the ground from Mamun camp on up and over the Indian–Pakistan border. The whole area was 'alive'. We were given tea and small eats as we wandered around, talking to JCOs and soldiers, all smiling and alert and seemingly interested in meeting a British officer who could speak reasonable Nepali. A small group of pipers played.

We went to the JCOs' mess for lunch, before which a Subedar Majors' Trophy was unveiled: this is an upright square white board, on legs that has on it oval discs of the heads and names of all subedar majors of the battalion since 1815. Quite how the trophy will be used I did not learn. After lunch I again wandered around and found myself once more an object of curiosity, in particular with the retired Indian-domiciled Gorkha officers who had, probably, never met a British officer before. One question I was asked was how I managed without butter and jam in Nepal – quaint! – and my knowledge of the 'tribal' language I had greeted the subedar major in had been overheard and had spread like the proverbial wildfire. A great talking point!

That evening's programme started with the army motorcycle daredevil display. Outstanding, not only ten on one bike but four men playing cards, the foremost man facing backwards, were amongst many other skilful acts. After them the pipes and drums appeared from behind a screen and gave a most polished performance. The pipers did not march straight but swayed from side to side, which was a novelty, at least for me. Even more so was when they and the drummers started dancing, squatting down and jumping up, blowing and drumming the while. Quite awesome.

A kukri dance followed and it was during that that I suddenly remembered what had lain dormant for over half a century: the only time I had seen a man cut with that knife was when I was with 1/1 GR, north of Saigon in Cochin-China in late 1945, when disarming the Japanese. I was the quartermaster when, one morning, I took a vehicle down to the market to buy fresh vegetables and a Viet Minh rolled a grenade under our vehicle. As it exploded the driver jumped out and chased the thrower. As he reached him the man lunged forward and the kukri missed his head and messily took off his right buttock. Needless to say, we didn't buy any vegetables but instead brought the man back to camp. I had thought I had behaved with a tinge of bravery but got a severe rocket instead ...

The sun had set and it was night. The pipes and drums emerged once more from behind the screen. Cords on uniforms were lit, red for the pipers and green for the drummers, with the regimental badge on the big drum shining blue – bodies otherwise dark shapes. Almost surreal but, in its way, I was captivated.

Being on the cusp of becoming a nonagenarian, I was, by now, knackered, to put it mildly. Buddhiman vetoed my going to the run up to the actual bicentenary eve programme and told me to go to bed. I therefore missed the cake cutting, the release of bicentenary balloons, the inauguration of the bicentenary trophy that, similar to that already mentioned for subedar majors, has the heads and names of all commanding officers, British and Indian, since 1815, unveiled at midnight minus eight, followed by – on the stroke of midnight, as the 200 years 'happened' – the dedication of the bicentenary song. I was singularly sorry not to have been there but my absence was, of course, commented on and understood.

On the second day we had a memorial service, a guard of honour, a group photograph and a special *sainik sammelan* (military gathering) in a large hall. On the stage were, on one side, previous colonels of the regiment and on the other previous commanding officers. One sign of senescence is that even such elderly people look so young! Two pipers and two riflemen armed with naked kukris escorted Lieutenant General Ravi Thodge, with Colonel Sandipan Bhattacharyya, the CO, and the oldest one-time subedar major on to the stage. They sat in the middle: the two riflemen, facing outwards at ground level, stood to attention without any movement during the forty-four-minute session, wrenching my heart strings with delight at their impeccable posture. I felt proud of them. Ubiquitous and undiluted panache was a constant.

In the afternoon a band concert was given, conducted by three different people. The playing was excellent and everybody enjoyed it.

Later, in our room, our liaison officer brought in a large paper container, suitably inscribed with the battalion badge and the 200 Glorious Years motif. Inside was a plethora of goodies, including a red silk choker, with the badge and 1815–2015 written underneath, a large wall clock, with a regimental badge with new logo and a coloured outline of a Gorkha soldier on its face, a blue baseball hat similarly inscribed but without the background soldier, a pair of cuff links, a tie clamp with a soldier's hatted-head motif, a container of first aid medicines, a box of 'emergency' buttons and thread, and an embadged butterfly broach, suitable to put on a lady's sari. Such a bounty was unexpected but most welcome: I can only presume all officer guests were given one each. Later I was given a suitably inscribed commemoration medallion. What careful planning had gone into it all!

A symphonic evening in the officers' mess was followed by a bicentenary dinner, and after the outside guests had gone, around 10.30 p.m., only 1/1 GR officers and wives were left. We were on a lawn and the fierce heat of the day had ebbed. Each of us had to come out in front and speak. I had brought two of my books, suitably inscribed. One was *Jungle Warfare* and the other *Gurkha Tales*, the last article of which was the letter I had sent to the CO after our 175th anniversary celebrations. I started by quoting a song of sadness of parting that took me back to when I left the battalion and how it had always been part of me. I said that I had written about the 175th anniversary so that the 'outside world' could learn about it and that I hoped to follow up with another book with an article on the 200th anniversary. I told them of when, forty years and one month after leaving the battalion, I was walking across the then-open Pokhara airfield when an old Gurung soldier saluted me, saying he, too, had been in 1/1 GR. I had asked him his regimental number: he had almost forgotten the one he'd had under us. '2394,' came his answer. It was now my turn to think. 'Your name is Tulabahadur,' I replied. It was. His expression did not change when I got his name correct. 'A battalion is an extended family,' I explained to the assembled company. The other time of applause was when I said that, during the difficulties of getting citizenship, it was ex-JCOs of 1/1 GR not ex-any of the British Brigade of Gurkhas, who led delegations to the Home Ministry in Kathmandu to help me in my quest.

We eventually got to bed at 2.30 a.m.: the others stayed on till 6, had a drink of tea and departed. Later on that morning we drove out for a picnic; on the way we heard about the earthquake in Nepal. A sad ending, indeed, to what I wrote to the CO on my return:

'The event of a lifetime', such that had never happened before and can, certainly for me, never happen again. I have seen five 'round-eye' armies and ten Asian armies: I doubt if any of them could have reached the standard that your battalion did during those three action-filled days. It was marvellous to meet so many new Indian officers as well as meeting those we had met in 1990. Indeed, as our men have it, personal contact is the pollen of friendship.

Mere words cannot do justice to the intensity of my praise for all your personal and the battalion's efforts for making the 200 years' celebrations unique, probably in the history of the Indian Army. The amount of work and planning that had to be done for such a splendid show boggles the mind and makes adequate thanks and appreciation, however sincere, seem incomplete.

Not only all that but the smartness, cheerfulness and all-round efficiency that was everywhere palpable left me almost breathless and, at times, with tears so hugely inspirational was it, as was the pride in unit that shone from your soldiers' faces …

The journey back was more tedious than on the way there as we had to change trains at Lucknow and wait on the platform – crowded, noisy and hot – for eight hours, sitting on a hard bench. At 4 a.m. the next morning, on crossing the border back into Nepal, unlooked-at and unnoticed, I laughed once more. Five minutes later, tongue a-twitch for a glass of hot sweet tea, the smile left my face when the brew we were given had, by mistake in the dark, been made with salt.

Yet, as Tennyson has it in *Maud*, 'Ah, Angel Memory who can/ Double the joys of faithless man', for me, as well as, surely, all those others who were privileged to attend such a wonderful, once-in-a-lifetime anniversary programme, memory will follow what Tennyson wrote, while, of the eight-hour wait on Lucknow station platform, it has halved that of an unrelieved numb bum.

Final Thoughts of an Old Soldier

So there you are! Congratulations if you have managed to get through that lot! Of course, there is much more but 'enough is enough is enough'.

You will most probably have noticed that I have not touched politics; the vexed question of 'differentials' in pay and pension; or the Tripartite Agreement – not 'treaty', which originally was quadripartite with East Pakistan allowing, or not, Gurkhas on leave and termination of service to carry kukris when using its railways; what Prime Minister Pandit Nehru said in the Lok Sabha about the use of Gurkhas by the British and their being allowed passage from Nepal, first by rail to Calcutta for onward passage to Malaya, Singapore or Hong Kong, then by overflight; or change in terms and conditions of service when soldiering in Britain and Brunei became the norm; or any other similar concern.

Of course, such matters are import, but they do not capture the flavour of soldiering nor living with the people of Nepal. During my nearly thirty-eight years of army service in Asia, I came across five what I wrongly call 'round-eye' armies – British, French, Australian, New Zealand and USA – and ten Asian armies, including Japanese, Royal and secret Thai, Royal and secret Lao, North and South Vietnamese, Malay, Singapore and Brunei. I have also seen students from all five continents undergoing training when I was first the chief instructor, then commandant, of the British Army's Jungle Warfare School. I know, gentle reader, you will tell me that comparisons are odious but I have always seen four types of problems in armies: officer-to-man relations; working under pressure; reacting to the unexpected; and having problems that seem to have no answer. It is their awareness of these four aspects of soldiering that, in my mind, have made the Gurkhas unique in the three armies in which they serve, British, Indian and Nepalese, as well as the Gurkha contingent of the Singapore Police Force, and, probably, the Sultan of Brunei's ex-service Gurkhas. I maintain that, when properly trained, properly led, properly equipped and properly armed, the Gurkhas are the world's best soldiers.

I finish with what I first carved, in 2003, on to the birdbath next to Buddhiman's private temple in our compound in Pokhara. It marks my silver jubilee with my surrogate family. I had it re-carved on becoming a Nepalese citizen. I want to share with you its message:

I became a Nepali in my 90th year but I was born a Briton, a direct descendant of Cadwallon, King of the Britons, AD 656, himself a direct descendant of Joseph of Arimathea. I have found more love and happiness with my Nepali family and friends than I had ever thought possible. It is my everlasting wish that this same love and happiness will also forever be found between the people of Britain and Nepal, especially in my surrogate sons, daughters, grandchildren and for all generations thereafter.

The words written here are also written in my heart and no one can rub them out.

7 Kartik 2071 BS
14 November 2015
Lt Col J.P. Cross
OBE FABI MCIL BA (Hon.) (TU)

Index

INDEX

You may also be interested in …

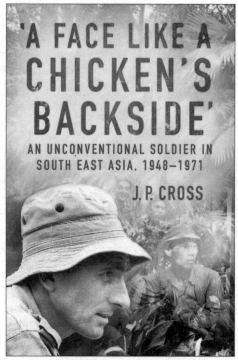

'A FACE LIKE A
CHICKEN'S
BACKSIDE'
AN UNCONVENTIONAL SOLDIER IN
SOUTH EAST ASIA, 1948–1971

J. P. CROSS

978 0 7509 6437 1

'This is the best book about jungle fighting I have read … Men like Cross win
battles.'
Major General R.L. Clutterbuck CB OBE
Royal Society for Asian Affairs